NEVER FIGHT WITH A PIG

A Survival Guide for Entrepreneurs

NEVER FIGHT WITH A PIG

A Survival Guide for Entrepreneurs

Peter H. Thomas

Macmillan Canada
Toronto, Ontario, Canada

Canadian Cataloguing in Publication Data
Peter H. Thomas, date.

Never fight with a pig: a survival guide for entrepreneurs

ISBN 0-7715-9139-X

1. Entrepreneurship.   2. Success in business.
I. Title.
HB615.T56 1991   658.4'21   C91–094520–9

1   2   3   4   5   FP   95   94   93   92   91

Cover design by Libby Starke
Cover photo by Derek Norris
Cover illustration by Raymond Chiu

The title of this book does not constitute a direct or indirect reference to anyone named in the book.

Macmillan Canada
A Division of Canada Publishing Corporation
Toronto, Ontario, Canada

Printed in Canada

Contents

Dedicated to the memory of my mother
Trude Thomas
1914–1981

Preface

Never fight with a pig.
You can't win.
You both get dirty.
The pig loves it.
— Pasquale Capozzi

You might wonder why I would choose *Never Fight With a Pig* as the title for this book. My answer is simple: It sums up many lessons that I have had to learn during more than two decades of entrepreneurship.

The primary issue you face as an entrepreneur is conflict. You are constantly dealing in a world that is exciting but dangerous if you allow it to get to you.

I have witnessed many business casualties along the way — entrepreneurs who became addicted to their businesses and couldn't deal properly with the day-to-day challenges. They couldn't separate the necessary conflicts from the useless ones and they have paid a price, losing their health, their marriages and some even their wealth.

The biggest lesson in this book is how to travel the path of the entrepreneur and win the spoils of battle without becoming stressed out and without losing objectivity because of an over-sized competitive ego.

The truth is simple — never fight with a pig — never

allow yourself to lose sight of your goals and become involved in needless conflicts or hassles that provoke you. If winning will only help you "get even" or "show them who is right" and the victory comes at all costs, it isn't worth it. You can avoid most of the unpleasantness in business by avoiding conflict and people who cause it.

The title does not refer in any way to any individual mentioned in this book. It is intended only to describe the importance of avoiding negative side issues and losing your objectivity. Remember, you don't need to win every battle — just the war.

Acknowledgements

Never Fight With a Pig is the product of over thirty years in the business world, twenty-five of those as an entrepreneur. Although the bulk of the book deals with lessons learned through direct experience, a great deal of what I know today was gleaned from a fairly relentless program of self-education — attending countless seminars and workshops and reading everything I could get my hands on. This book draws together the best of the ideas I was exposed to over the years, with memorable quotations from these talks and publications that I have noted in my Personal Goals and Values Guide. Although I have indicated herein any words that are not mine, in most cases I have no idea where I got them. They are published without attribution but with gratitude to those who taught me so much. I would be pleased to receive any information regarding the proper identification of sources.

Introduction

Freedom is the absence of necessity,
coercion, or constraint in choice or action.
Total freedom requires absolute discipline.
— excerpted from Peter Thomas's Personal
Goals and Values Guide

My mother, Trude, was a young, well-educated, single Austrian girl from a wealthy family who found herself pregnant and alone when Hitler invaded her homeland in March 1938. With the aid of distant relatives in England, she was able to flee and find work as a nanny in the household of the Haig family, of Scotch whisky fame. She carried all her worldly belongings with her in one bag, which was snatched off a train platform in England as she waited to catch a ride to her new home; she arrived at the Haig residence with literally nothing but the clothes on her back.

It was there that I was born in September 1938. To this day, I know next to nothing about my natural father.

England was not the best place for an unwed mother with a German accent. After the war my mother was courted by a Canadian soldier, a truck driver named Robert O'Brien Thomas, who held out hope of a new life in what seemed like the promised land. When I was seven years old they married and we left London for a remote farm outside Perryvale, near Athabasca in northern Alberta.

There are two things I remember most about those early years in Canada: how hard my parents worked, from before dawn until midnight, and how the school-children ridiculed and attacked me for my short pants and British accent. I was a tough, difficult child because I was determined to make my own way and never accept anything from anyone, especially someone who wasn't my "real" father.

I was so hard to manage as a child that I became the bane of the existence of my school principal, who never missed an opportunity to grab me by the ear and shake me, saying, "Peter Thomas, you're never going to amount to a hill of beans! You'll never make anything of yourself! There's nothing you can do right!" I'll never forget that man's name: Victor Laskosky, Principal of Perryvale Central School. Probably most people have at least one Mr. Laskosky in their lives, someone who managed to convince them of their worthlessness. Fortunately, I had the opportunity to meet Mr. Laskosky at a recent school reunion and let him know that he miscalculated.

The way we respond to such criticism is a crucial aspect of our development. Whenever this type of comment comes back to haunt me from my youth, I just remember what Bette Midler said when she was asked how she rated herself on a scale of one to ten: "Fifteen!"

To pay for my books, bicycles and movies I undertook many entrepreneurial ventures, including shooting squirrels for their skins. At age seven I sent away through comic book advertisements for information on selling greeting cards door-to-door, and made quite a bit of pocket money that way. During the early years it was my responsibility to split all the wood for the winter for

two houses, ours and my grandparents', and my grand-
father paid me for his share.

I started picking blueberries and selling them along
the Alaska Highway when I was very small, and did it
until I left home. Often I would lead the American
tourists off the highway to remote patches where they
could pick their own berries, charging them five dollars
for the directions. Of course, these patches belonged to
local people, particularly one Mrs. Wolver. She didn't
mind folks picking in these areas, which would never
have been touched otherwise, but one day she took me
by the hand and led me back to where the tourists had
been. They had brought in very crude boxes with nails
fastened to them called "blueberry pickers," which had
mangled the bushes so badly that they were rendered
useless for bearing fruit. Thereafter I quit "selling" Mrs.
Wolver's blueberry patches. That was my first lesson in
entrepreneurial accountability.

When I was twelve I started working in the sum-
mertime in the co-op store twenty miles away in
Athabasca — just long enough to earn money to go
water-skiing for the rest of the season. One summer I
learned that a new sewer line was being put down in the
town, laid parallel to the sidewalks, and that it was the
homeowners' responsibility to dig the ditches for it. I
approached a couple of owners to ask how much they
would pay me for a contract to do the job, and found I
could get as much as $250 at each house.

I went to the hardware store and bought ten shov-
els. Then I headed down under the Athabasca Bridge,
where local Indians would often sleep in the summer. I
convinced a group of them to work for me on an hourly
basis, and signed up a slew of contracts. At my peak I
had five ditches being dug at one time.

One day when I was hard at work at one ditch I glanced up to see an Indian who had been digging at another site racing down the street toward me, yelling incoherently. I ran back to where he had come from and, much to my dismay, found another man in the ditch buried up to his armpits in wet, stinking clay. Apparently he had broken through a rotten septic tank and fallen in. The wet sand all around the tank had caved in on him.

We dug frantically, found a rope and eventually hauled the poor guy out. But in the turmoil one of the neighbours had called the local authorities. When they discovered that I was just a kid who did not have a registered company and was not a licensed contractor, they shut me down.

I never accepted a penny from my parents until the day I left home at fifteen to join the army, when my stepfather gave me a hundred-dollar bill as I headed out the door. By then I was a pretty wild young man, full of unbridled energy that ricochetted off everything in its path. It was not unusual for me to go into a bar determined to get roaring drunk and find myself a good fight. If it weren't for the self-discipline I learned in the army, I might have continued to go through life as an accident waiting to happen.

Those who know me often shake their heads and glance heavenward when the subject of my self-discipline comes up. Once I learned about discipline in the army, I realized that it would allow me to focus on a goal and achieve it. At all times I carry a briefcase — really a zippered time-and-information organizer in a three-ring binder — that has become like a second skin. It literally contains my life: my appointment book, important phone numbers and my daily regimen, among other things. It used to drive Nelson Skalbania crazy to see me take that thing with me wherever I went. But there is nothing more important to me than a disciplined, balanced life that neglects neither the professional nor the personal values that are spelled out in my Personal Goals and Values Guide, which is also in my briefcase and which I add to whenever I see something worthwhile.

That discipline is the key to my success, the ultimate goal of which is increased personal freedom.

The formative experience in the army that stands out in my mind was in 1959 when I was sent, as a member of the Royal Canadian Dragoons Reconnaissance Squadron, to the Suez Canal to help man the armistice demarcation line between Egypt and Israel. The United Nations had drawn a line through the desert that no one was supposed to cross. Anyone who dared was imprisoned without trial.

Try telling that to the Bedouins. They had been roaming this desert freely for thousands of years and didn't comprehend modern refinements such as international borders and property ownership. They also carried, hidden in the folds of their many layers of clothing, knives that could slit your throat in a second.

It got to the point where there were so many people in custody that there was nowhere to put them. One night when I was on guard duty high atop a four-foot-square tower above our encampment, yet another Bedouin was rounded up. The duty officer decided that since there was nowhere else to put him, he could go up in the tower with me.

It was two o'clock in the morning. I was a young man from rural Alberta armed with a Bren gun, famous for its ability to fire off an entire magazine with one slap against a door frame. He was a nomad who may or may not have possessed a knife.

I pointed my machine gun at him and then swung it toward the tower. He understood, and up we went. He crouched in one corner and I crouched opposite him in another, no more than three feet away, with the gun pointed at his head. I was terrified — there was no doubt in my mind that if he blinked or moved, I would shoot him. And he knew it, too. We stayed that way, without moving or speaking, until six in the morning. I consider that experience to be my introduction to negotiating skills.

When I left the army it was early 1961, I was twenty-two and I could shoot and I could type. Neither of these skills qualified me for the fast track in Calgary, so I headed for the bush, where high salaries could be earned by anyone willing to endure remote locations. I got a job as field accountant (which meant I looked after the payroll) and safety engineer (which meant that I had passed a St. John's Ambulance first aid course), first with Flint Rig Corporation and later with Stearns-Rogers Engineering Corporation, both of whom were building oil and gas installations in northern Alberta. My first stop was Whitecourt.

Right after I returned from the Suez, and before my discharge from the army, I had fallen in love with a seventeen-year-old Calgarian named Donna Cotton. We wanted to get married, but her parents refused their consent — required by law because of her age. They didn't like me much; I was brash and smooth talking, with a penchant for big cars and booze. But Donna sulked for so long after I left Calgary that her parents finally gave in. She showed up in Whitecourt with a suitcase full of stuffed animals and moved into my boarding-house room. We got married the same day in a nearby Anglican church with two hastily arranged witnesses for company.

Donna had to go to work right away, since I made only $800 a month, and $500 of that I owed for my new car. (Donna recently calculated that during our twenty-five-year marriage we owned a total of 250 cars at one time or another; they were the only expense I ever considered essential. I had even worked part-time as a mover while I was in the army in order to pay for a car.) As soon as we could we moved up in the world — we rented a trailer.

When I went to work in the Alberta bush, I had to work hard to earn the respect of the men on the sites. I was the man from head office who was responsible for safety, but to them I was really just a kid. Stearns-Rogers in particular prided themselves on their impeccable safety record, which they expected me to uphold.

At one of my first jobs, at Pincher Creek, Alberta, a worker got a steel splinter in his eye. He staggered up to me with the splinter sticking out of his eyeball, jamming his eye open.

I just looked at him. The situation called for instant action and all I had was my first aid kit. The civilized world of doctors and hospitals was many many miles away. And the St. John's Ambulance course had not included a lesson on splinters in eyeballs. I was on my own.

I rummaged around in the first aid kit and discovered a little plastic loop. Hooking it around the splinter, I just yanked the piece of steel out. After packing the eye with a gauze bandage I sent the worker off to hospital in Calgary. I don't know what became of him, because he never came back to the job site. But I'll never forget that first time I had to take responsibility and make an instant decision.

Later on at Lookout Butte, Alberta, I learned never to be intimidated by anybody. On that site was a construction worker named Indian Joe, who along with other Natives used to work atop the oil rigs and gas plants, building the highest parts. Indian Joe was the ringleader of a group determined to give the greenhorn from head office a hard time.

One day an order came down that no worker was to take off his shirt, no matter how hot it got, because there were too many injuries and days off from sunburn. The day that announcement was made, I came out of my office — really just a shack — and looked up at least one hundred feet to see Indian Joe high in the sky, standing on top of the steel girders. He stared at me and I stared back. The riot of construction noise stopped and the whole site came to a standstill as all eyes turned toward us.

Slowly, Indian Joe unbuttoned his shirt, took it off, and let it float gracefully to the ground.

Without saying a word, I turned around and walked back into my shack. I was shaken, because I didn't want a confrontation and screaming match with Indian Joe, and I didn't want to lose a valuable worker. But I couldn't simply let the incident go.

I told the secretary to make up Indian Joe's paycheque and deliver it to the foreman — the construction worker was fired on the spot. When the foreman got the cheque he tore into my office shouting that I couldn't do such a thing, but I stuck to my guns. From that day forward I have operated on the conviction that if you feel strongly about something you should do what is right, regardless of other people's reactions.

That determination to operate on my own terms
has motivated me to this day and has created the business advice you are about to read. I've made a lot of
mistakes along the way, both personally and professionally, and tried to learn from them. It is that education that I am sharing with you here. My values and my
attitudes have altered radically, as you shall see. My
stepdad and I are friends now, and I'm considering
taking a new career path. A lifetime of discipline has
brought me to a secure place in the world where I now
have the freedom to do whatever I please. That is the
biggest thrill of all.

On August 13, 1990, the *Financial Times of Canada*
published a special supplement called "The Entrepreneur: The Top 100 Growth Companies." Number one
on the list was Samoth Capital Corporation — I am the
majority shareholder of this publicly owned merchant-
banking, real-estate-management and investment company, listed on the Toronto Stock Exchange. It would be
dishonest to deny that it makes me proud to have come
this far from where I started, after many ups and
downs. But through it all I have maintained my conviction that success has nothing to do with money. Success
is the attainment of a predetermined goal; failure is
nonattainment. That goal could be absolutely anything
you choose, from the most banal and ordinary to the
most grandiose. In order to achieve those goals, you
need to have the courage to examine critically, and if
necessary ignore, other people's rules and make up
your own.

For me, success is being able to tell my grandchildren, when I am seventy-five years old and they ask me

what I did with my life, about a wide range of experiences. I want to be able to sit them on my knee and tell them about doing as many different things as a person can possibly do — that is what success is to me. It is certainly much more than one career path or my net worth.

And one more thing, something I can say to myself every day: "Mr. Laskosky, you were wrong."

ONE

Learning from Your Mentors: My Years with the Men from Principal

Almost anything you do will seem
insignificant, but it is very important that
you do it.
                    — Mahatma Gandhi

Sergeant Preston of the Yukon is credited with say-ing, "The view only changes for the lead dog." By the end of my five-year tenure at financial wizard Donald Cormie's First Investors Corporation of Edmonton in the 1960s I had decided that I was going to be a lead dog. I made a resolution that guides me to this day: Never be enslaved by someone else's plan — create your own.

After leaving home at fifteen and doing a seven-year stint in the army, I bounced from one odd job to another. Finally, at age twenty-five, I realized that I had better get serious about a career.

The year was 1964 and I was working as a carpen-ter's helper at a firm that built Quonset huts. Using steam heat, we moulded wood into curved units. It was gruelling work and one day I looked around me and saw the reality of my fellow workers for the first time: they were grown men in their forties, fifties and sixties doing the same three-dollar-an-hour job that I was doing. I knew that if I didn't get organized I could end up just like them. Not long after that I answered a newspaper ad for sales-manager trainees at First Investors Corporation.

When I signed on in 1964, First Investors was a ten-year-old investment contract company with about twenty regional offices nationwide and assets of $50 million. It was the first of the companies that Donald Cormie would unite with several others two years later to constitute the Principal Group. There were only three other such organizations in the country. Twenty years after my departure, the bankruptcy of First Investors led to the collapse of the Principal Group — which by then included thirteen investment companies — and the loss of the personal savings of 67,000 Canadians.

First through savings certificates and then through mutual funds, First Investors and later sister companies invested people's savings, primarily in mortgages as well as in securities (stocks, bonds and the like), earning customers far more interest than they could as single investors. Essentially, it operated the way insurance companies do, except that it provided savings without insurance. The salesman's job was to sign on customers for any of a variety of these savings packages for a commission. Regional and district managers received override commissions on the sales as well.

The savings companies in the group offered a guaranteed fixed rate of income on their certificates. The mutual fund companies professionally managed pools of money that were invested in securities, so income fluctuated; the value of each investment unit in a mutual fund was determined by the total worth of the investments divided by the number of units in the fund, which continually offered new shares and stood ready to redeem existing shares. There was also a trust company in the Principal Group; it operated like a bank, with all monies available on call. The savings plans we sold provided access to the full range of investment services offered by all the Group's companies.

When I started, I was a kid with no skills or experience outside the army and the odd jobs I'd held since then, and First Investors put me through an intensive series of sales-training workshops before they sent me out on the job. My motivation to work hard came during my first year at the company when I brought home a $7,000 cheque representing one month's commission on sales of guaranteed savings plans. I put the cheque on the bed between my wife and myself and sat there, stunned by the amount of money it was possible to make if only I put my mind to it. Up to that time I had been merely an adequate salesman. After that day I worked toward the goal of being the best in the business.

I was a young man who had not yet found a mission in life to which I could harness my unbridled energy. The day I brought home that $7,000 cheque, selling became my mission. I had finally found something that would reward the kind of single-minded dedication and strong self-discipline I was willing to throw into a job.

I earned that $7,000 cheque for one month's work by making the most of an unexpected opportunity. One of the salesmen I had hired was despondent because he just couldn't make his quotas, and I decided to take him on the road and show him how the job was done — a practice I have used frequently to motivate and train staff. Since he was from Hanna, Alberta, I took him there.

When we arrived in Hanna, the salesman went to the Legion hall for a beer, and I found myself alone in a seedy motel room. The man in the room next door had left his door open and sat working away furiously at his calculator. I struck up a conversation, only to discover that he was the accountant who prepared the tax returns for the farmers in the area.

The wheels started turning in my head. We continued talking, and before we knew it we had come to an arrangement whereby I met his clients when they came in to pick up their returns and offered my services to them as a business consultant. Next morning I sent the salesman back to Calgary to pick up all the necessary forms, and I set up shop in my motel room. I called my boss, General Sales Manager Ken Marlin, a man who was to become my lifelong friend and mentor, and told him to send a cheque for $10,000, charged to my account, over to Tom Durham, owner of Interprovincial Accounting, the firm that employed the accountant; I asked Ken to tell Tom that there would be more where that came from.

During the next few days the other salesman and I sold savings plans that provided farmers with tax breaks that they never would have had otherwise. I shared the commission with the accounting firm and the salesman, so it was really a $21,000 commission that was made in that time.

Once I had decided on my mission, how did I achieve it? I looked around to see who the best performer in the company was, and modeled myself on him. I studied everything he did and made sure that I did it too. Then I bettered that person — I went one step beyond him in my performance. That meant topping his sales record and earnings, first as a salesman and later as a manager.

By the end of my second year with First Investors I was the top salesman out of approximately two hundred in the firm. I went to Ken Marlin and said, "What's next?"

The next thing to do in the company was to sell mutual funds, so I learned that.

Again I asked Ken the all-important question, "What's next?" and the result was that I became a district sales manager. In 1966 I was named top district manager out of about forty at First Investors Corporation. The following year I was the top regional manager of the twenty managers nationwide, and became general sales manager of a sister company, Associated Investors of Canada.

It is important to set reasonable goals, and when those are achieved, set new ones. When I was in the army I never wanted to be the general, but I always wanted to be one rank higher than I was. The same principle applies to the workplace. It was easier to believe in myself and to avoid the disappointment of failure if I kept my goals realistic, but kept upgrading them.

My goals were achieved through some very unusual business practices that may not work for everyone. You may have to create your own unorthodoxies when you chart the path to your goal. For instance, one day I created and sold a savings plan that wasn't part of the packages being offered by First Investors. They had monthly and yearly plans for various sums of money, but they had no plan for investing an amount as high as $2,500 annually. That day I just invented the plan and wrote an order for it. The manager at head office hit the roof, but eventually the sale was completed.

As an added bonus from my profitable trip to Hanna, Alberta, Tom Durham, the owner of the accounting firm, became a close friend and an early inspiration to me. *His* first job had been as a coal shoveller on trains, stoking the engine's fire. One day when he was particularly sick of the job, his supervisor came along and started yelling at him as he worked, claiming he wasn't performing fast enough. It was the last straw for young Tom. With his final load of coal, he threw the shovel into the fire and hopped off the train.

Tom was another who believed in being creative if that's what it took to achieve his goals, and he told me stories of his bushpilot days, when he had a contract to transport furs and fish from northern Alberta to southern markets. Once he had the brilliant idea to bring in fish directly from Great Slave Lake to Edmonton wholesalers, circumventing the fish brokers and making much more money. So he filled a boxcar with frozen fish and sent it on its way. To this day, that boxcar has not been found.

Somewhere on a smelly siding in Alberta is that load of fish. The story taught me that it doesn't pay to try to outsmart people who know better than you what they are doing. Question authority but learn to discriminate between those who know what they are doing and those who are simply following old habits or are plain incompetent.

On one flight through a raging storm, Tom was carrying not only fish but also an Inuit with his sled and dog team. In the midst of the storm, with the plane fumbling and bouncing its way south, one of the dogs chewed its way loose from the harness and started attacking Tom, growling and biting his neck. He reached under the seat, pulled out a monkey wrench, and swung at the dog — who managed to duck. Tom accidentally clobbered the Inuit, who passed out and fell forward onto the wheel. The airplane went into a nosedive.

Tom managed to recover control and all survived. He was more careful about his modus operandi ever after. It was a lesson I learned the hard way at the Principal Group.

Ken Marlin loves to tell the story of the day I marched through the front door of his home at six in the morning, while he was still shaving. I headed straight for the bathroom, parked on the toilet seat and proceeded to eagerly spell out my latest scheme for increasing sales before my stunned and half-naked boss. Finally his wife, Helen, came into the bathroom and asked if I could please put my career on hold until her husband had finished shaving.

Another time Helen nearly threw me out of the house. I was invited over for dinner, but as soon as Ken and I arrived he got a long-distance phone call. It didn't take long before I was pacing the floor and demanding to be served, Ken or no Ken — I had a business appointment to keep. Helen Marlin told me I could wait for Ken or I could leave now.

One time I was sent to Victoria to investigate an office that wasn't producing enough revenue; it also had funds that mysteriously went missing. When I got there and assessed the situation, I realized that the problem was the manager. So I fired him, and called Ken to tell him what I had done. "So what are you going to do now?" Ken asked incredulously. I had no idea who would fill the job and reorganize the office. I was immediately appointed Victoria branch manager and was instructed by Ken not to leave until I had replaced myself with a fully trained manager. It was three months before I got out of Victoria.

I will never forget the time I sat in mindlessly on a staff meeting while Ken delivered a long-winded speech about a major promotion he was about to make. He talked about a very talented employee who had been with the company only briefly but who had made a major contribution, and who stood out as the obvious candidate for the job of assistant general sales manager. I was sitting there not paying any attention, thinking about going out for a beer with my buddies after the meeting. When he announced that the new assistant manager was Peter Thomas, I nearly fainted with shock. I had no idea that it was going to be me. The move not only kept me happy, it stimulated me to even greater challenges. It also encouraged others to follow in my footsteps.

Ken protected me in my third year when I demanded that the company throw out the rule book and give me my own division to manage. My immediate supervisor was ready to fire me, because I had not yet proven myself by recruiting, training and supervising staff for him. Ken kept telling me that the rules were that I had to demonstrate that I could attract and develop good people. And my supervisor wanted the override commission due to a manager on all his staff's sales — he wanted a piece of my action. He was waiting for me to become his hiring machine, so that he could take his commission. But I insisted on my own division, even though I had very little management experience.

Ken interceded; he allowed my superior to save face by letting him retain the override commission and by making me pay my own way. Then Ken gave me enough rope to hang myself: my own little division office on 14th Street in Calgary, a secretary and permission to build a sales force. First Investors didn't even pay the rent.

I didn't care how much money my former boss made off me. I was determined to work on my own at any cost. Within six months that little office was the top division in Canada. I brought in some really gung-ho guys who were out to lick the world.

My take-charge attitude was not restricted to the business environment. My ex-wife, Donna, says that I was a super salesman at home as well as on the job — I could always convince her to see the world from my point of view, to make my dream hers. So when in my single-minded dedication to achieving financial independence I decided that it was not important to have furniture in our first real house, we had little other than beds. I simply felt that our money could be spent in more fruitful ways and I didn't believe in personal credit purchases — except when it came to my cars. Furniture could come later, when we were so well-off that we wouldn't miss the money — when we could afford the best. The children like to tell people that they remember when we had lawn furniture in the living room; little do they know that we had it only because I had won it as a bonus for being the top salesman. And we didn't own the house. It has never been important for me to have one, which is why when we moved to Victoria in the mid-1970s we ended up living in a posh hotel suite for fifteen years.

Obviously my youthful obnoxiousness has had to mature into a more sophisticated way of doing business. Today, I feel I have an iron fist with a velvet glove over it — people usually don't realize how aggressive and persistent I am. That's the sort of style you need to get people to cooperate with you in any aspect of life and work, but particularly if you're an entrepreneur.

Before its collapse in 1987, the Principal Group included thirteen companies marketing savings, investment and retirement plans, and First Investors was one of those companies. In 1985 authors Paul Grescoe and David Cruise called one of them, Principal Trust, "the fastest-growing financial institution in the country." It was the only organization in the world where you could buy, supplement and borrow from mutual funds through an automatic teller machine. The Principal Group had the first Instanet computer in the country. Through it the companies traded stocks as fast as anyone on the exchange floor, and produced share certificates from anywhere in the world via computer printout. The group was famous for bang-on maverick economic forecasts that eventually made Donald Cormie worth over $200 million.

Mr. Cormie — he always was and always will be Mr. Cormie to everyone he works with — was the financial genius and prime mover behind the Principal Group. He was a Harvard Law School-trained lawyer and represented the elite of the western Canadian business aristocracy; his was one of the most powerful families in the province. He had a state-of-the-art, high-tech, 14,000-acre cattle ranch and was a partner in the prestigious Edmonton law firm of Cormie Kennedy. From the time he took control in the mid-1950s, he ran the Principal Group from his law office until he acquired his luxurious quarters atop the new Principal Plaza. In those days he was a trim, attractive man who could have been the model for the actor who played J.R. Ewing in "Dallas." Alberta at the time was Canada's version of J.R. country, and Mr. Cormie ran the Principal Group just like a modern-day king of the financial cowboys.

First Investors was started in 1954 by Stan Melton of Melton Real Estate. Mr. Cormie was Stan Melton's lawyer. Originally there were five major shareholders, each with 15 percent interest, and a few with smaller amounts — thirteen shareholders altogether. Gradually Mr. Cormie bought out all the other shareholders except Ken Marlin, who eventually held 10.5 percent interest. Ken, the soft-spoken and gentle founder of Marlin Travel, is a humane man who has the management and marketing skills Mr. Cormie lacked, and he was essential to the operation. That's why Mr. Cormie allowed him to be his only shareholder in the end — he wanted to nail Ken's foot to the floor.

Donald Cormie's genius lay in his ability to develop to perfection the relatively new idea of private contract savings companies, of which there were never more than four groups in Canada. He pioneered the exploitation of the latest technology and his eccentric economic forecasts were nothing less than oracular. Mr. Cormie also developed a marketing team that not only put a winning plan in place, but selected and honed front-line men who were zealots. The linchpin of the success of the Principal Group was brilliant marketing, and no matter what the Group's onerous failings, there is not a marketing whiz alive who could not learn from Principal.

I learned all my basic sales skills from the people who trained us there. Mr. Cormie's concept of thrift — of saving religiously and building up an untouchable nest egg — has become the foundation of my philosophy. I learned many other lessons from him as well.

I was sent to Seattle in 1966 to establish a sales office. As soon as I had done the legal paperwork and sold some plans from my hotel room, I called back to head office to ask for money to run the operation. Mr. Cormie simply told me, "That's what you're there for, to make sure I don't have to spend money. You're supposed to find the money, or find ways to do without it." I didn't get the cash. We solved seemingly insurmountable problems of staffing and starting up an office without any money.

Most people who set up a new operation have huge cash-flow needs. But we let our sales activity dictate the kind of operation we could afford, and we never did need to put money into the organization. We didn't open a big office at the beginning — we didn't have an office at all until I had drummed up enough sales to pay the rent; instead I continued to work out of my hotel room. Then I found a hole-in-the-wall office to work in until we had a sales pattern in effect that allowed us to afford better premises.

I followed exactly the same pattern when I left the Principal Group to start my own business. I opened a tiny office in the Edmonton suburbs that was only big enough for three people, with no secretary. I worked there for almost a year before I hired my first full-time secretary — Patricia Nicholson, who is now vice-president of Century 21 Canada.

From that trip to Seattle I learned that talented people were the key to success. If I had talented people, I didn't need to spend money on a posh office and classy stationery — the talented people I hired would generate the income for those things. The only start-up investment necessary was the money to bring those people on board and keep them there.

On another trip, when Mr. Cormie and I were on an airplane together, I took advantage of the opportunity to seek his advice. I was making $50,000 a year at the time, and I asked him to tell me how I could earn $200,000 a year. He told me that he couldn't tell me that because I wasn't ready. He said to come back to him when I was making $100,000 a year. When I got to that point, however, I didn't need to go back — I knew how to do it without asking. The experience drove home the point about setting goals that I knew exactly how to reach.

I learned to set goals that I personally could visualize attaining. If I didn't have the knowledge or skills to achieve the goal, I had no business setting it for myself — or others.

During my years at Principal, I not only picked up top-notch sales skills and the confidence to go out on my own, I also learned what not to do as an entrepreneur, manager and employer from watching Donald Cormie. As sure as he was the key to the success of the firm, he was also the key to its failure.

Mr. Cormie always said that a ship could have only one captain and he was it. He didn't like having minority shareholders because he didn't want to be accountable to them. Although he had a brilliant business mind and a superior marketing program, he was an unyielding autocrat who brooked no interference. He certainly had no place for ambitious upstarts like myself. Everyone who worked for Principal knew that they had to be sure that Mr. Cormie approved of all their actions in advance. From him I learned some of the pitfalls to avoid when I became an entrepreneur myself.

THOMAS'S TIPS

1. *Listen to the people around you and go with your winners. Don't be a one-man show.*

    Going to a meeting with Mr. Cormie was like standing at attention as a general instructed his troops: he spoke, you listened. He did not welcome new ideas from others, or accept advice from them. If Mr. Cormie had had the wisdom to listen to others, the Principal Group might have survived with its integrity intact.

    When I came up with a plan to service workers at the new Fort McMurray tar sands with a new company that would run a mobile bank in a converted bread truck, it was shot down immediately; in the meantime, another bank was offering a similar scheme to remote communities elsewhere in Canada.

    Consulting others is an integral part of the business process, especially when it comes to compensating for your own shortcomings. My staff consists mostly of people who are information gatherers who do a sniff test to assess any deal before I get involved. And before I commit to anything, I bounce the deal off a trusted second — a different person in each case — who will temper my enthusiasm with sobering advice. I tend to get excited about projects too quickly, and I know I need someone to check my impulses and play the bad cop.

2. *Delegate both responsibility and authority.*

    Mr. Cormie seldom delegated authority. You have

to establish a way for your employees to earn more authority, and allow them to make mistakes.

A corollary to this rule is this: Don't be afraid to let your talented people acquire equity in your projects, because that will give them an added incentive to stay with you. It also gives them a personal financial interest in a project's success. Equity motivates peak performance.

3. *Get the right kind of loyalty — don't be a taskmaster.*

Everyone at First Investors would do anything to keep Mr. Cormie happy — they were terrified of him, and that was their main motivation. They would do nothing to risk his displeasure; they were nearly all yes men — including myself, as long as I wanted to stay on the team.

The right kind of loyalty includes having people around you who will tell you in your own best interests when they think you are wrong. They work hard for you because they respect you and want to do their best for you. When you speak to your employees, it is important to let them know that you will make the ultimate decision, but you want them to tell you everything about a project or a problem, both the good and the bad. They must feel that you respect their judgement and that they are free to say what they think without recrimination.

4. *Cultivate interpersonal skills in addition to business skills.*

Mr. Cormie was like a radio transmitter that only

sent; not only did he seldom receive incoming messages, he rarely established a rapport with his workers. When the chips were down, almost everyone — with the exception of his immediate family — abandoned him, and few sympathized when he fell from grace. Never forget that the people involved in a project are more important than the project itself, and the art of motivating the talented people you have selected is the most important skill to have in any successful venture.

At one staff meeting, Mr. Cormie told the sales force that he could sell certificates more cheaply by selling them directly across the counter — leaving staff with the impression that they were all going to be fired. We had a difficult time motivating people after he'd told everyone that he didn't need them.

In retrospect, the best thing that ever happened to me was Donald Cormie's refusal to let me be a shareholder. I became the top regional manager in the company in 1967 at age twenty-nine and that's when I crossed the Rubicon: I decided that I wanted to be a shareholder in the Group. By that time I was general sales manager of Associated Investors of Canada, one of the companies in the Principal Group. I'd learned by then that you don't get rich on sales commissions, you get rich on a piece of the action, and I felt I'd earned the right to buy it. When Ken Marlin heard the idea his knees went weak; he knew how Mr. Cormie would respond. But in my usual fashion, I stuck to my guns: I wanted shares or I would walk. I was certain they would never let me go.

Ken insisted that he would set up the meeting with Mr. Cormie and that he would come along for the ride, but I had to make my case on my own. Cocky as ever, I was sure I could ace it. I prepared my presentation with great care, and at the appointed hour we went across town to the august legal offices of Cormie Kennedy.

When we walked into Donald Cormie's pristine, uncluttered, wood-panelled office, the experience took on the aura of an audience with the Pope — and I was there to espouse the virtues of Protestantism. Ken quickly gave a recitation of my achievements over the past four years and said that I would like to talk about acquiring shares in the company. Mr. Cormie cut him off with one soft-spoken sentence: "If he wants shares, Ken, you can let him have some of yours."

It was like a bullet passing through me. Ken leapt backward visibly. I had never been defeated before and for the first time I learned what it is to miscalculate badly. Donald Cormie didn't care if I stayed or went. I never did get to make my presentation.

In retrospect, Mr. Cormie was shrewd enough to know he could never keep me happy; I would always be wanting more. As Ken Marlin likes to say, I came in at the bottom of the company and went out at the top. I was really meant to be running my own operation — and I was lucky not to be at Principal when the tragic end came.

Shaken but undaunted, I immediately gave one year's notice of leaving the company: I would be gone in November 1968. Then I made plans to go into business for myself. I gave such long notice because I still could not believe that they would really let me go. What's more, the Principal Group was the only working life I had known — I needed very badly to get my act together. And I needed a year's grace to start my own operation.

I had learned another lesson the hard way: it is important to have Plan B at all times, to think strategically and weigh the options. I had learned all my professional skills at the Principal Group. I had no idea what I was going to do. The only thing that was obvious was that I was not going to fit into someone else's agenda.

During my years at the Principal Group I developed marketing skills that I have continued to refine to this day, as the deals got bigger and the stakes higher. From Ken Marlin I learned how to manage people and motivate them, both as employees and customers. "Keep leaning and smiling" is a favourite phrase he used to describe the body language of selling that has stayed with me. He taught me to empathize with customers by having me memorize the following poem:

> To sell John Smith
> What John Smith buys,
> You must see John Smith
> Through John Smith's eyes.

Twenty years after I stopped working for him, Ken is still my friend and adviser and he played a pivotal role in my decision to withdraw my offer to purchase Heritage USA.

I was lucky to have as a boss a man who both appreciated my talents and tolerated my faults. Ken Marlin recognized people's special skills and made it his job to learn how to exploit them, while at the same time protecting all concerned from their own shortcomings. It is important to have someone like that in any organization, especially for an employee on the way up. If there isn't a good mentor in the workplace, ambitious employees will find a new place to work.

It was a shock to me when the Principal Group, by then worth $1.2 billion, collapsed in 1987 and Mr. Cormie's multiple bookkeeping was exposed at the Code Inquiry into the scandal. The hearings revealed that the company's auditors hadn't received complete information; there was allegedly a breakdown in the audit trail. That breakdown affected a total of $367 million in initial investments and over $100 million in credits and interest.

When I was with the company in the 1960s, our sales force functioned like messiahs, saving the world and solving its problems with the wonderful products and services Principal offered. I never questioned the safety of our customers' money. That wasn't an issue.

To this day I do not believe anything dishonest was going on while I was there, and I am convinced that if it happened, it began to happen at a later date, only because the Alberta economy took such a terrible downturn. When interest rates rose in the recessionary early eighties, people started defaulting on mortgages, which jeopardized the investments of some companies in the Principal Group. And when the Alberta government unceremoniously pulled the plug on two of those firms, people started hauling their money out of all the companies, including the securities-based ones, making collapse inevitable.

But when push comes to shove, it was the boss who was responsible. Mr. Cormie failed in my opinion because he thought he was so strong that he could do anything. He thought he was invincible — he was the perfect example of the King Arthur Syndrome. If you are a fabulously successful person whose economic forecasts have always been right and whose command of technology is brilliant, and if you have never accepted anyone's counsel before, why change now? Aren't you savvy enough to outsmart a little bit of recession?

Ultimately, in my opinion, Mr. Cormie decided that he would stare down the Alberta government. He would not comply with their needs — he would make them comply with his instead. The government's responsibility was to protect investors by creating regulations for this new industry. Mr. Cormie, of course, had his own ideas about how the industry should be regulated. Most businessmen prefer as little regulation and disclosure as possible and the Principal Group lobbied particularly for generous income-averaging allowances. Mr. Cormie was frustrated at the government's lack of understanding of the business, as well as its refusal to grant the industry the same operating terms as banks and insurance companies.

In the early 1980s the economy was in terrible shape; it was a bad time for all western-based financial institutions — Alberta had lost a few already — and the provincial government was desperate to save Mr. Cormie's floundering investment companies. They would have done anything within reason to keep Principal going. As the Code Inquiry demonstrated, they allowed the Principal Group to continue to operate in a business-as-usual manner long after its financial position began to weaken, in the hope that the economy would recover. The two parties also came to an agreement eventually on income-averaging, so that the group's annual reports continued to indicate a healthy corporate body.

Mr. Cormie had an armada of lawyers and an

incredibly powerful personality; his family was steeped in Alberta history. When he faced a bureaucrat in the Alberta government, Mr. Cormie struck fear in him; it was like taking on a Kennedy or a Rockefeller. But the timing was totally against him; the economy just kept getting worse and worse.

The Principal Group didn't turn into a nightmare overnight -- it takes years for that sort of financial collapse to happen. What the management team did wrong was that they never acknowledged the fact that their assets were depreciating and altered their operations accordingly. We all have a tendency to put off bad news in the hope that good news will come.

The managers at Principal should have cut their overhead dramatically, rented out some office space and invested more of their own money in the savings-certificate companies — they should have added capital to replace what had been lost on mortgages. If they had increased their capital base and cut costs, recognized the real value of the properties they had acquired through default, and been honest with customers, they could have secured new investors at a new base, on revised terms. But they waited too long to deal with reality.

Ken feels strongly that in spite of all this, if the government had allowed the Principal Group and other investment companies to operate on the same basis as the life insurance companies and banks under the jurisdiction of the Superintendent of Insurance, the disaster never would have happened. By law, these institutions are allowed to use an eight-year averaging system in assessing the value of their investment portfolios; that way the recessionary write-down can be balanced against the value of these assets in the good years preceding and following an economic downturn. Ken and Mr. Cormie had lobbied strongly for such a change to the legislation. The companies were, after all, operating in all other respects exactly as life insurance companies do.

By 1984 Mr. Cormie and Ken had reached an agreement in principle with the Alberta Superintendent of Insurance that they could calculate Principal's worth in this fashion. It was on this basis that their annual report was issued and that their licence was renewed. Yet the determination of the Code Inquiry was that they had committed fraud in publishing figures in 1984 showing that the company was viable. The problem was further exacerbated by the fact that responsibility for investment companies was transferred to the provincial Treasury Department, which had no staff familiar with the workings of such companies, shortly after the deal was struck with the Superintendent. Ken and Mr. Cormie had to start lobbying and negotiating all over again.

Beyond that, collapse could have been averted, according to Ken, if Principal, the last independent financial company in Alberta, had been supported financially by the provincial government, which had done so in other cases.

Even when the licences for First Investors and Associated Investors, two of the thirteen companies in the group, were lifted, he feels it could have happened without investors losing a penny if the Alberta government had maintained public confidence in the other eleven companies by demanding that the shareholders pledge all their assets in support of government backing for the two troubled companies. What they did instead was lift the licences of the two companies and announce the action in such a way that it looked as if the whole group was bankrupt. The resulting media coverage destroyed the confidence of investors and the public in general. It also destroyed the value of the assets of all the companies in the group when investors panicked and started a run on their money — precipitating the devaluation of investment certificates and the collapse of the Principal Group.

That move, as well as the Code Inquiry and the criminal charges, seemed precipitated by political motives. The objective seemed to be to get public officials off the hook, and skewer scapegoats. If the objective had been to secure the investors' money, the licences would never have been lifted in this fashion.

Ken Marlin was particularly shaken by the collapse of the Cormie empire. Unbeknownst to most people, he lost his rightful share of the holdings. Ken stuck with Mr. Cormie until the sordid end, and had been unaware of the creative bookkeeping that was revealed. Ken says that he could tell that something strange was going on, but he had no concrete evidence.

Not until the day in October 1987 — two months after licences were lifted for two companies in the group — when Diane Stefanski, Mr. Cormie's personal bookkeeper, walked into Ken's office and, as he puts it, "spilled her guts." Among other things, she told him that on Donald Cormie's instructions she had wired $4.2 million in Principal funds out of the country.

Ken had no access to the books for the Principal Group's parent company, Collective Securities Limited — that was Mr. Cormie's private domain. However, a reputable accounting firm showed good receivables for the public companies in the group, so he believed the auditors.

Ken is truly the tragic figure in the collapse of the

Cormie empire. He's a man who has been tarred with the same brush as Donald Cormie himself, to the point where in July 1989 he was charged with fraud under the federal Competition Act by the Department of Consumer and Corporate Affairs.

In the meantime, he endured the Draconian style of Donald Cormie, who consistently refused to buy out Ken's interest in Principal, forbade Ken to run Marlin Travel on the side (since 1976 Ken's son Rod has owned and run it) and denied his partner of over thirty years his rightful access to information. Ken also endured twenty-three months of the Code Inquiry. He has stated that he has lost millions of dollars in earnings that Donald Cormie's bookkeeping deprived him of, and he has lost his home.

At sixty-eight years old, Ken Marlin was an undischarged bankrupt with federal criminal charges pending against him and a legal-aid lawyer defending him. He and his wife, Helen, were surviving through the generosity of their children and friends, and through their indomitable fighting spirit. That is not the same fate that befell Donald Cormie and his Vice-President of Corporate Development, Christa Petracca, both of whom are charged along with him, and both of whom have suffered much less drastic changes to their life-styles.

Worst of all, those who trusted their investments to the Principal Group feel that Ken — in addition to Mr. Cormie and Ms Petracca — is primarily responsible for their losses. If that is so, it is only through acts of omission rather than commission. For Ken Marlin's story is one that demonstrates the limitations of relying on hard work alone.

Ken had had only one previous employer —

Canadian Pacific Railway, where he worked his way up from telegrapher to dispatcher — when he became a founder of First Investors Corporation in 1954. While at the railway he moonlighted as an Electrolux vacuum-cleaner salesman. It was through this job that he developed confidence in his business skills, and decided to look for an opportunity to develop a career in marketing. He thought he had found what he was looking for when he met Stan Melton and Donald Cormie. Together they built an empire.

From the very beginning of his involvement with Principal, Ken had all his eggs in one basket. Mr. Cormie wouldn't buy him out or let him diversify, insisting that he dispose of his interest in Marlin Travel, which he had founded in 1967. Yet Ken knew that if he walked away from the company, his 10.5 percent — his whole life savings — would be worthless. When the economy took a downturn and the mortgages that Principal had invested in declined in value, his salesman's creed told him that if he just sold more product, all the company's problems would eventually be solved. He felt that he could just sell his way through the economic trough, but he called it wrong — things stayed bad for a lot longer than anyone expected.

It is as important to manage an operation properly as it is to market it properly. If Ken Marlin is guilty of anything, it is the error of not asking the right questions and examining the whole operation in depth himself. He left too much up to Donald Cormie; whether he had much choice in that regard is the critical question.

If Ken's vision had been broader — if he had applied more than the marketing man's credo to the job — and if he had been the kind of person to know when to get in and when to get out of a venture, he might not be where he is today. His loyalty has cost him more than his 10.5 percent share: it has cost him almost everything.

Four years after the collapse of the company he spent his life building, Kenneth Marlin would like nothing better than to be quickly and summarily tried and judged so that he can get on with what is left of his life. He and his wife live in Richmond, B.C., where Ken managed a Handiman franchise for a short time.

In contrast, Donald Cormie's family lives in a plush mansion in fashionable Paradise Valley, Arizona. In a smart office in nearby Scottsdale, an affluent suburb of Phoenix, he and his son James and Christa Petracca run a "modest financial services company," according to Matthew Fisher in *A Matter of Principal*. Fisher notes that:

> Mr. Cormie presumably still has access to the
> $4.2 million that Diane Stefanski wired to New
> York for him just days before Principal Group
> collapsed. . . . The aging financier seemed to be
> leading a surreal "Alice in Wonderland" existence.
> Donald Cormie was said to be incredibly upbeat
> under his legal and financial situation and what
> the future held in store for him.

In July 1990 Ken Marlin sat beside his former partner in an Edmonton courtroom at the hearing that determined that the federal government would proceed to trial with charges against them, and Donald Cormie made a point of telling him that the Canadian government was pursuing him for back taxes.

"It was his way of letting me know," Ken practically whispered to me on his return to Vancouver, "that I shouldn't bother to sue him, because there probably won't be anything left to take."

When I left, Mr. Cormie asked me how I could leave a job where I was making over $100,000 a year. I simply said to him, "Mr. Cormie, I'm not leaving the job, I'm taking it with me. I created it."

There was some bitterness about that later because I ended up successfully suing Mr. Cormie for commission fees he owed me. I had a compensation arrangement that was different from that of all other sales representatives and managers; I had the title of general sales manager but received no salary as everyone else did — only a commission override on all sales that took place in my areas of responsibility. The commission on those sales continued to come in for several years after I left the company and I felt I deserved that income. Mr. Cormie was furious, because no one else would have dared to sue; no one ever stood up to him.

Once again I had flouted the unwritten rules of the corporate game, acting more like an entrepreneur than an employee. During my brief time with Mr. Cormie I was the brash new recruit telling well-heeled Old Boys of my father's age and older how to run their business. That kind of irreverence and an innate driving need to prove myself over and over again made me an ideal candidate for entrepreneurship. I built up a lot of self-confidence because I had been given the opportunity to play with the big boys. I had excelled at the game, and often won.

At the Principal Group I learned that while I was a good salesman, I did not make a very good employee. It was clear that it was time to strike out on my own. In retrospect, I would not have done anything from those days differently; in fact, I think I waited too long to move on. I established a pattern that I have taken with me all these years, and I recommend it to others: zoom in on a goal, find yourself a role model, study the business until you understand it thoroughly, become a clone of your model, surpass your model, and boom — you're gone.

Over the years I have refined my formula for success in any venture, but it was first tested when I left the Principal Group. It boils down to a system I detailed for *Achievers* magazine in 1989:

$$AMC + G \text{ (that RUMBA)} + H = Success$$

Attitude, Motivation and *Commitment* (AMC), are the most important elements of every single thing you do, whether it be social, family, business, health or finance. Get a positive attitude, make sure your motivation is there and get your commitment in focus, no matter what the project is. These elements are what make the entrepreneur a success; if you don't have a strong dose of all three, entrepreneurship may not be for you.

G is for Goals and RUMBA means those goals have got to be *Realistic, Understandable, Meaningful, Believable* and *Achievable*.

For your goals to be *realistic* means that you have to look at things the way they are. Realize you are not going to make money in the first two or three months of a new venture, perhaps longer. Are you going to quit the first time an ill wind blows? Do you have a bank account to tide you over? Marketing and selling are the best businesses in the world but people drop out because they don't plan an effective start-up strategy. They aren't realistic about what could happen. Keeping your goals realistic must be uppermost in your mind — the number-one consideration.

Your goals also have to be *understandable*. Do you understand what you have to do to earn $50,000 per annum? Do you understand what time you have to get up in the morning? Do you know what a day's work in your chosen business is? Do you know how to do it all?

After expenses, if the business leaves you with $25,000 per annum, are you going to feel happy about that? Is such a result *meaningful* to you? You have to have something that is meaningful to you to turn you on, to motivate you.

Also, you have to *believe* you can *achieve* these goals. You have to believe in what you are doing and your ability to do it.

The H stands for *Health* — you have to look after yourself at least as well as you look after your new venture, or your poor health may spell the end of it. And your health is affected by your personal life, your relationships with your family and friends.

Each day, check the above formula for success against your list of goals — intellectual, family, community, recreational and professional — to generate excitement about those things you enjoy. That excitement is the key to motivation. Whenever people who work with me distinguish themselves with top-notch attitude, motivation and commitment, I present them with handsome gold AMC pins in recognition of their achievement.

A way to test your understanding of your goals and how to get there is the practice of visualization, which functions on many levels. First of all, visualize yourself successful at whatever your chosen goal or venture is. Visualize the details of your life when you reach that goal. Keep that image in your mind as you plan your strategy — you will succeed if you are convinced that you will, and visualization helps to create that conviction.

Secondly, visualization helps you determine which deal to get involved in. You imagine the potential of a project down the road, as I did when I heard about an opportunity called Century 21, and you keep that image in your mind. Usually that means thinking creatively about options and possibilities that have not occurred to other people, options that challenge conventional business practice.

Creative visualization may also set off alarm bells about a particular project, because what you see happening down the road does not suit you or your operation. As I told *Vancouver Venture* magazine in 1987, you have to build on your strengths to be consistently successful in business innovation. You have to ask: Which of these opportunities fits me, fits this company, puts to work what I am good at and have proven myself at in the past? Visualization may well tell you that the project in question is heading for disaster, with or without your help.

I left Principal to set up my first business, Edmonton-based Western Diversified Holdings International. Some of the strategies I used to get this company off the ground in 1968 will apply to any first-time entrepreneur and indeed to any new venture.

Establish your new business before you quit your job.

I started dabbling in real estate while I was still at Principal. For my first investment I borrowed $9,000 from the bank to buy a house in Edmonton, and put $1,000 into renovating it and refurbishing it myself. I charged about $180 a month for the whole house. When I sold it I got $18,000 for the house and put the money down on a $55,000 apartment building. I fixed that up and sold it for $85,000. Both those transactions took place within ten months, and I'd earned $38,000. That's when I said to myself, "Peter, you'd better look seriously at this real estate business."

I read everything I could about who was doing what in real estate, and chose successful role models. I tried to come across concepts before other people did. For example, I was one of the first in Canada to sell real estate in limited and general partnerships, which has since become an accepted way of marketing real estate. I was the general partner and manager who bought the property and ran it on behalf of other limited partners who contributed cash only; profits and losses went directly to all the partners and not to the company, and tax benefits were divided among us as well. Projects were structured this way because of the benefits of having limited liability. The worst thing that could happen to investors would be that they would lose the money they had put into the deal; the limited partners would not be liable for any of the loans or mortgages if the project went under.

I also had securities salespeople selling property. They weren't licensed to sell real estate, and the real estate industry objected. But I argued that it wasn't real estate — it was a security. Then the securities commission came in and saw real estate brokers selling what the commissioners perceived as securities; but my lawyer, Neil Crawford, the former Attorney General of Alberta, successfully argued that my staff was selling pieces of buildings — real estate.

There were no laws to deal with this type of thing then. Back in the late sixties we were operating in an area that had not been defined in law. Today, the definition of a security in the Ontario Securities Act, for example, is two pages long. Now a security is any document ("instrument") that represents a financial interest in a company or other fund. Securities include everything from stocks and bonds to scholarship trusts, and even private transactions in which one party receives money in exchange for an investment document. Securities are regulated provincially and the vendor must adhere to a strict set of guidelines administered by a securities commission. Every time a new type of business enters a provincial jurisdiction, the commission must determine whether that business falls within their mandate. Real estate syndication and real estate franchising are two areas where there could be potential confusion: Is the vendor selling real estate (or franchises), or is he selling securities? Generally speaking, syndicates are considered securities but franchises are not.

Buy into a successful operation.

I bought 50 percent of the Western Growth Fund (WGF) of Edmonton, a well-established mutual fund company, and brought some of my own salesmen with me from the Principal Group. Under my holding company,

Western Diversified Holdings International Ltd. (WDHI), the mutual-funds operation merged with real estate, development and syndication companies to work together. My trusted second at the time was an accountant named Bob Chernick, whose job was to follow me around after I bought something and assist in the financing of the acquisition. Included in his job description was the responsibility to tell me that I was getting into a bad deal, or that it should be restructured. For the most part he negotiated the details of deals that I initiated, within the parameters that I laid out.

Make sure that the successful organization you buy into has as one of its assets proven, high-calibre people who can assist you in reaching your goals.

The board of directors at WGF were pillars of the community who became my next mentor group. Through them I cemented contacts that it would have taken me years to accumulate on my own. They included the son of the ex-mayor, Lyall Roper; a Queen's Counsel, George Bryan; the president of the real estate board, Jack Weber; and Dr. Eardley Allen, head of the famous Allen Clinic in Edmonton; through him I made contact with the doctors who would participate in my syndication deals. This acquisition in effect elevated my prestige in the community, which worked well both for my directors and for myself, because when I started to promote their interests, they could open doors for me.

Add marketing impetus to an old idea.

I noticed that some people were occasionally getting together in loosely connected associations to buy a piece of real estate. But no company in Canada that I knew of was doing it as a full-time business on a professional basis and I devoted a lot of time to marketing syndicates. I believe I was the first one in the country to make syndicating real estate a major part of my operation.

Through real estate syndication I built up Western Diversified Holdings International to a level that qualified me for membership in the Young Presidents' Organization (YPO). Mr. Cormie, who was a member, had introduced me to it when I was at the Principal Group. He went regularly to their conferences and brought back ideas gleaned from all the best and brightest young minds in the business world, and I paid close attention. I knew that it would be to my advantage to join as soon as I could.

In order to do so I had to be sponsored by a member. To qualify for sponsorship I had to be under age forty and be the president or chairman and chief executive officer of a company with at least fifty employees that did in excess of a specified volume of business per year, depending upon the type of business. The sponsor's nomination was subject to a vote of the membership.

After I joined in 1973, it was through YPO that I not only enhanced my skills but also learned about the deal of the century.

TWO

The Deal of the Century: Century 21 Real Estate Canada

> I believe that mediocrity is self-inflicted
> and that genius is self-bestowed.
>
> Every successful man or great genius has
> three particular qualities in common. The
> most conspicuous of these is that they all
> produce prodigious amounts of work. The
> second is that they never know fatigue,
> and the third is that their minds grow
> more brilliant as they grow older, instead
> of less brilliant.
>   — Warren Russel, *The Man Who Tapped the
> Secrets of the Universe*; excerpted from Peter
> Thomas's Personal Goals and Values Guide

It is well known that there are four key aspects of marketing — people, communication, financing and timing — and if you are good you can control the first three. Financing is the easiest of all to accomplish. Timing however is usually a matter of luck, and when I bought Century 21 Real Estate, a lot of luck was with me. I wasn't a genius — if I hadn't done it, someone else would have.

I first heard about Century 21 Real Estate at a Young Presidents' Organization conference in Hawaii in 1974. I had been sitting at the beach in Honolulu with Forrest Olsen, a major California real estate agent. He told me about his friend Art Bartlett, who was franchising real estate brokerages. He was packaging advertising, hiring and training services with a national image and offering the package to small real estate brokers for a percentage of their commission. It seemed like a crazy scheme to me, but the more I listened to Forrest the better it sounded. I felt a rush of adrenaline go through me as I grasped the concept: multiplying income at brokerages through national marketing services — once again adding marketing impetus to an old idea. In fact, it combined two old ideas: real estate and franchising. Soon I was brushing off the sand, placing a phone call to Art Bartlett and leaving the conference for Los Angeles on the first plane I could catch that day.

It was not luck that put me on that plane to California to clinch a deal for the Canadian franchise territory; that's called seizing the opportunity. The lucky part was that the timing was perfect.

When a new business is launched, the most important thing to assess is the timing. I've seen lots of people go broke because they didn't analyze the timing, and if it was wrong, say no.

Many times the person who introduces the public to a new concept doesn't get the sales. The consumer has to be educated. For instance, consider fax machines. If a salesman had offered you one when they first came out, by the time he had explained what they are, you'd have been tired of listening to him. You would probably have had no interest in buying one. Now, you couldn't do business without a fax and you don't need to be talked into getting one.

Real estate brokers across Canada had been familiar with organized real estate for several years. When I went into business in 1976, over 50 percent of the people I approached knew of Century 21 because of their travels to the United States to real estate conventions. At the same time, some American advertising for Century 21 reached across the border — today probably 20 to 30 percent of the company's advertising is free in Canada because of that border-hopping. And competitors had already been out there ahead of us talking to Canadian realtors about franchising — there were schemes in place in some provinces already, such as Realty World.

When I went out to sell the Century 21 concept, some of the tough educational years were already behind the industry and Century 21 was the most visible of the franchise schemes. It also had the most to offer; it was the most organized out of the chute. Like bucking broncos, we were out there ahead of the rest of them — just that little bit, not too far. If you get too far ahead you die.

Once I had decided that the timing was right, the part of the deal that I had to negotiate hard for was the territory. I had to convince Art Bartlett to let me have Canada, because he wanted to sell me British Columbia only. On the one hand, Canada is almost a throwaway to American business people, because the market is so much smaller that they often don't take it seriously. But I had to come up with terms and guarantees that would encourage Art to let me have the whole country. I agreed that I would sell 120 franchises in the first three years. My self-imposed rules were that I would not open for business in Canada until I had sold twenty franchises in one territory and I would only sell to qualified brokers who had been in the business for at least five years. These were my criteria for choosing the people I would work with in Canada. They reflect the realistic, modest goals important to any new venture.

The next thing to settle was the financing, and I decided I wouldn't do the deal with Bartlett unless I could get the rights to Canada for $5,000 down. When a business is starting up, it is important to base any deal on the smallest possible down payment, especially when the risk factor is so high. It was going to be a long time, if ever, before I saw anything but expenses from Century 21 Real Estate. It took me about three months to do my risk assessment, or due diligence, which included checking the parent company's books and travelling all over the United States to personally assess the success of the franchising. I discovered that the situation was even better than Art Bartlett said it was.

When we finally nailed the deal down, Art and I scrawled some almost illegible stuff on the back of a pad of paper, signed it and ripped off the corner of the cardboard. It was a binding contract, and it hangs, framed, on my office wall today.

What that scrap of cardboard said was that I purchased the rights to Century 21 Real Estate Limited in Canada for $100,000, with a $5,000 down payment. The balance was financed at 6 percent over ten years. It proved to be one of my best investments ever.

Next we had to develop a strategy for setting up operations. The most important factor was location. I was still in Edmonton at the time, and decided that the Century 21 concept required a larger population base for its first shot. Toronto I felt was too big and competitive; it was the hardest nut to crack, so I decided against it. Besides, it was too far away from my base of operations at Western Diversified. Montreal was even farther away and it meant dealing with language problems. We opted for Vancouver, the third-largest city in the country; it was close to Edmonton by air and had a wonderful climate and environment.

The first thing I did was move to Vancouver and begin talking up the idea to British Columbian realtors. I was the communications department and I put 125 percent of myself into it. I knew that my best skills were communications skills — selling — and that if I devoted myself to selling Century 21 Real Estate, it would fly. Once I settle on a market, I chase it as if my life depends on it — I consider that to be one of the pillars of my entrepreneurial wisdom. My plan was to sell twenty franchises in this territory and then have an opening breakfast celebration. It was a pattern the company would follow consistently in every territory.

Next I looked around for the best real estate agent in town for the job of selecting prospective brokers and managing the franchises. I wanted a hard worker who could demonstrate a high rate of success, and who would know the best local dealers to bring into the system. After making a few phone calls, I knew that the person for the job was a man named Uwe (Gary) Charlwood, a German-born, British-raised immigrant who ran Hunt Realty Limited in North Vancouver. I phoned him, and after three months of negotiation he came aboard. Gary bought the first franchise sold in Canada, and we agreed that he would be the executive vice-president of the company. He turned out to be the perfect man for the job — and because he was the perfect man, our relationship became, unfortunately, an example of the classic entrepreneurial dilemma.

Gary and I lined up twenty excellent franchise sales prospects, and Century 21 Canada Ltd. opened for business in 1976, but not for long. We were struck immediately by a crisis that could have destroyed the whole thing. Word came down from the B.C. Securities Commission that I did not have authorization to do business. The Commission ordered us to suspend operations so that it could undertake an investigation to assess whether we were "selling securities without a licence." Eventually I had to let my Century 21 staff go, and I went back to what I knew best: buying, selling and syndicating real estate.

Gary and I waited for six months with no progress. I was new in British Columbia. I had absolutely no connections, and had no idea how to go about convincing the regulators that I was selling franchises, not securities.

One day I was making my way through the Vancouver airport terminal, preoccupied with the subject foremost on my mind: legal clearance to start my business in Canada. As I walked past a bank of pay telephones off to the left, I looked at them and, for some strange reason, visualized Jimmy Pattison's face. I had once met the millionaire entrepreneur, now known as the man who ran Expo 86, on one of my earlier business trips to Vancouver when I was still selling real estate out of Edmonton. I knew that he was a go-getter and resolver of problems. He was an action-oriented individual who could give me the type of advice I needed.

I went to the phone booth and located his number. I managed to get him right away, and told him my story. He thought about it for a minute and asked where I could be reached. I gave him the number of the pay phone.

"I'll have someone call you immediately," he said. "Stay by the telephone."

I hung up and just stood there in the middle of the

airport, waiting. Sure enough, the phone rang within a few minutes, with Jimmy on the line: "Call Michael Butler. He's a well-connected securities lawyer in Victoria who knows his way through the legal labyrinth of the provincial government. He'll get you the clearances you need."

I did and he did — it worked like a charm. Once Michael Butler heard the details of my predicament, he announced immediately that there was no case; it was preposterous to suggest my franchises were securities. I called the staff back in and we were off and selling within thirty days.

Unbeknownst to me, behind the scenes the major B.C. real estate brokers had raised a ruckus when I had first opened up. I believe they pressured the government to stop my encroachment into their territory. What I was doing had never been done in British Columbia before, and the dealers pressured the Securities Commission to make Century 21 a test case determining if real estate franchises were in fact securities. But the real object was to delay the decision so long in the provincial bureaucracy that I would eventually pack my bags and go home.

Michael Butler ensured that the government came to a swift decision. He convinced the Commission to rule that real estate franchises were in fact not securities. Without him there might never have been a decision. In the end I didn't need a licence after all.

In retrospect, I had been a naive young upstart from Alberta who had been too intimidated by the whole process to even think of getting a lawyer on the case. I simply waited for the bureaucrats to give me permission to carry on business. The real agenda eluded me completely until Michael Butler stepped in.

The lesson, however, was not lost on me: I should never surrender the power to control my own destiny. I should never wait for permission to do what I want to do, assuming that someone else knows better. Whenever someone tells me "No" there is usually a way to make it "Yes," no matter how far-fetched, if only I can imagine it and dare to do it. That's called visualization.

This wasn't the first time I'd had to call on visualization to make this operation fly. When I first bought the rights, my banker, Jim Watt from the Toronto Dominion Bank, didn't think it was a good enough opportunity to lend me money. He couldn't see California gold blazers working in Canada. My accountant, Colby Quilliam, said that real estate agents in Canada wouldn't pay me a fee merely for the proposed services; he advised me against proceeding with Century 21 Real Estate, and he wouldn't invest, either. I asked Ken Marlin to be my partner, and he said that although he thought it was a good idea, he was too busy at the time to get involved.

One day in 1975 Nelson Skalbania and I were driving across the Oak Street Bridge in Vancouver in his Rolls-Royce Corniche convertible, with the top down. I asked him what he thought of Century 21 Real Estate, and I'll never forget his reply.

"How do you expect to sign up a bunch of losers and have them pay you money? The small brokers are having a hard enough time now. They'll never be able to afford it."

Finally I asked my wife, and she said that she didn't think anyone would wear those gold jackets.

What none of these people realized was that Century 21 *could* work. The organization's high profile would increase the gross sales of all the small operators so that they could afford to pay us our 6 percent service fees. Franchisees could double and triple their grosses in two or three years — which is what they did. Everybody I talked to looked at the real estate business the way it was, not the way I could visualize it — the way it was going to be.

Never look at any project the way it is; visualize the way it can be.

When I made the deal to sell Century 21 in 1988, there were just under 400 Century 21 Real Estate offices in Canada employing almost 8,000 people. The company was the largest real estate organization in the country.

In 1984 *Canadian Business* magazine, in "The Education of Peter Thomas" by Wayne Lilley, noted that there were many sceptics when I first started up, and that one of them was Gary Charlwood. Gary initially signed on for a 10 percent share, he told Lilley, "only if I ran the company completely. Peter didn't know anything about the real estate sales business."

There is no doubt in my mind that Gary was material to the success of Century 21 Real Estate — that's why I hired him, and that's why I sold the first franchise to him. The entrepreneur's role is to evaluate opportunities, choosing the type of business to be in and the goals and objectives of that business. The next critical task for an entrepreneur is to find the right person to manage the business. The skills required to exploit new opportunities are not the same ones required to run the day-to-day operation of them. Hiring the right people, motivating them to do their best and delegating as much responsibility as they can handle will ensure the success of a new business.

In the founding of Century 21, I stuck to this model. I completed the acquisition of the franchise territory and made the critical decision to start the national franchise in Vancouver a full six months before I met Gary Charlwood. When it was time to find a chief executive officer to run the company, I looked for the best individual for the job and several indicators pointed to Gary, whom I had never met. He was hired as executive vice-president on the condition that he must buy a franchise. To this day I consider the greatest sales feat of my career to be the sale of that first franchise to Gary Charlwood.

Gary became a shareholder in 1977, when the company had been running for almost two years. At Gary's insistence, an amendment to our shareholders' agreement specified that I could not call myself the founder of the company; he and I had to be "co-founders." I didn't care what he called himself, as long as he got the job done.

Think about it — if you could delegate 75 percent of the work yet take away 75 percent of the profit, wouldn't you? As long as my bank account is full and I don't have to go into the office, I'm more than happy for Gary Charlwood to take the credit for the success of Century 21.

Public comments such as the one Gary Charlwood made to *Canadian Business* reveal an underlying tension that characterized our relationship from the beginning and was probably inevitable. It was the classic confrontation between a strong-willed, hard-driving entrepreneur, who was full of wild and crazy ideas but had very little desire for detail on the one hand, and on the other a hardworking, take-charge administrator who looked after the details. I was the front man — the motivator,

communicator and public-relations person who culti-
vated the corporate image and strategy, developing new
avenues for expansion and profit; Gary got the day-to-
day job done.

I knew that having me around was driving Gary
crazy, so soon after the business was in full swing I
moved out of the offices and into my own corporate
headquarters. It might have been good for staff morale
but it didn't do much for our working relationship,
which was polite but cool.

The relationship heated up in 1980 when I discovered that Gary was starting up Uniglobe Travel using
the corporate staff and facilities of Century 21. After
consultation with lawyers I decided not to take legal
action. By mutual agreement, Century 21 acquired a 10
percent interest in Uniglobe. But the relationship was
never the same.

PRINCIPLES OF DEAL MAKING

The deal for Century and the deals I've done since then
have allowed me to refine some of my principles of deal
making. Once you've found your opportunity and
decided that the timing is right to go after it, there are
some important things to remember if the project is
going to be a success.

> Keep your thoughts positive, because your
> thoughts become your words.
> Keep your words positive, because your words
> become your actions.
> Keep your actions positive, because your actions
> become your values.

Keep your values positive, because your values become your destiny.
— excerpted from Peter Thomas's Personal Goals and Values Guide

Although the above sentiments may echo your memories of Sunday school lessons or Boy Scout meetings, they provide a guaranteed route to successful deal making. Keeping things positive is the only way to win.

The AMC formula will help you define your goals and spot an opportunity; visualization will show you if it's a deal you should go for; now you need to prepare yourself to negotiate the best deal you can get. I have developed some pointers over the years that I have used. None of them is original to me — experienced deal makers will be aware of most of them. I have, since my Century 21 days, tried to give them each a little twist to make them work that little bit better.

Think of yourself as a risk assessor, not a risk taker.

As I told *Vancouver Venture*, when it comes to real estate investment excellent returns are to be found in the early stages of organizing and assembling a development project, not in holding and managing property for long-term capital gain or income yield. At Samoth Capital Corporation, our risk assessment tells us to stick to developments in their early stages and to focus on their earnings potential during those stages. In each case we determine the potential for resale and identify prospective end users. The goal is to acquire and merchandise land and buildings to realize a predetermined profit within a specified time for each investment.

I invest primarily in no-risk investments such as

46

Treasury bills and high-risk areas such as private companies, new concepts and start-ups. This is where I differ strongly in my investment practice from the common wisdom of financial advisers. I divide my investment money equally between no-risk and high-risk investments, whereas most advisers would caution you to stick primarily to low-and medium-risk areas. I put very little into Triple-A preferred shares and debentures, Dow Jones companies and prime real estate; I improve real estate projects through zoning, renovation or other means to the point where it becomes prime property and then sell.

Century 21 Real Estate was a high-risk investment of $5,000 that turned into an $8-billion per-annum business. It was leveraged without capital risk. Today approximately 50 percent of my money is in secure Treasury bills, and 50 percent is in real-estate-related investments. At Samoth Capital, we secure the principal in an investment and take an option or percentage of the profits in return for arranging most of the funds required to acquire, renovate or develop a property.

If you decide to do a project that is away from the city where you grew up in business — where you are well connected and familiar with the infrastructure — be sure that you do it in a place that you enjoy.

If you have to manage a bad deal, Hawaii would be a good place to do it, because you won't mind spending a lot of time there. Not all of your projects are going to go well, so you had better make sure that they are in a place where you wouldn't mind spending a lot of time while you clean up the mess. Inuvik might not be as good a place to do a real estate deal as Hawaii.

Three members of my staff at Samoth Capital Corporation and I are transformed regularly into a SWAT team to do risk assessment. We swoop down on a major city for a short time to assess its potential for investment and growth. In the spring of 1990 we went to Phoenix and Dallas. In each case we spent two days initially in the city and met with the city fathers, the chief economists and the chairmen of the chambers of commerce and the local banks, the head of the real estate board and leaders of the business and financial communities, including local developers, top real estate lawyers and middle managers at banks. We gathered information from libraries, clippings files and economic studies and drew up a report on the economy in each city, which we call a "snapshot" of the market. On the basis of these snapshots we decided in mid-1990 to focus our attention on the Dallas/Fort Worth area. We determined that it is currently one of the most attractive regional markets in North America. We decided to take a wait-and-see attitude toward Phoenix.

Both areas went through a boom in the early eighties followed by a slump. In Dallas, oil was driving the market; in Phoenix, it was Sunbelt hysteria. The Savings and Loans (S&Ls) gave away so much money that both regions overbuilt and their markets crashed, taking the S&Ls with them. Vacancies were at 60 to 70 percent in some cases. The oil market also took a nose-dive in Dallas, but there they restructured the economy by attracting new business that did not rely on the oil industry. In Phoenix they had not, as of 1990, been able to fill all the buildings that went up in the eighties.

Once you've gathered the information, you still have to go with your gut.

The point is that we try to identify the risks and minimize them as much as possible before we commit to an investment. We prefer the conservative approach of heavily researching both the assets and the people involved in any deal we are contemplating. We are investors, not gamblers.

Now that I have said this, I don't want you to think you should never take risks. The secret is to quantify the amount of risk you will take. An example I always think of is two of the records that baseball player Babe Ruth set. He was the king of baseball with 714 home runs to his credit, which every fan knows. But his other record was 1,330 strikeouts in his career — more than anyone else at that time. Babe just stood there swinging, knowing that when he connected the ball would go out of the park. To be successful in business you need to have the intuition and perseverance to keep swinging, but don't expect to hit home runs every time you go up to the plate. In other words, don't gamble with large, non-refundable deposits on every proposition that comes across your desk. You will not be successful with most of them.

Your job as an entrepreneur is to spot new opportunities early and then put together the talent and management to bring them to fruition.

The entrepreneur always searches for change, responds to it and exploits it as an opportunity. You have to identify the changing or fast-growing sectors of the economy. New growth opportunities rarely fit the way industry has always approached or defined the market. We were successful with Century 21 not because of myself or because of Gary Charlwood, but because I recognized that the real estate industry in Canada was ripe for change.

Before you enter into a new project, calculate first how you will get out of it.

As I told *Vancouver Venture*, in each case we want to know up front how we are going to liquidate an investment — which includes a realistic evaluation of how long we will hold the property as well as our profit expectations. The profit will be earned through a combination of value added as a result of reorganizing or dividing the property, leveraged buying and/or syndicating all or part of the project to outside investors.

Visualization helps me to determine at the start of a project, before I undertake an acquisition, exactly how I am going to divest myself of it in the future. If I can't visualize that, or if what I see looks too difficult, I don't go for the deal.

A few years ago I bought a hotel in Victoria for $2 million and put $1 million into fixing it up and building up its business. The structure had sat in receivership for four years. We changed the name from the Olympic Hotel to the Carlton Plaza Hotel and sold it within a year for $7 million, plus a management contract. The people who bought it have sold it again for $9 million. It was a case of looking at a seedy, run-down, neglected property and recognizing the potential in it that no one else saw. We changed its image and spruced it up for the tourist trade in Victoria.

If it is a longer-term project and you are going to operate in partnership with someone else, you should still plan for the end at the beginning; always have a buy-sell clause in your partnership agreement, as I did with Gary Charlwood. Business moves so fast these days that even though you and your partner are in love when you are doing the deal, three weeks later you might not like each other so much. It is much easier to have a premarital agreement that sets out the terms of separation than to go through the divorce courts. If there is a closing date for a deal ahead of you, make finalization of your buy-sell agreement a prerequisite to closing. If you let that closing date go by, then you end up with no clear way out of potential problems. Before closing, you will both want to have a clear idea of what happens when one partner wants to buy or sell; after closing, perhaps only one of you will be interested in casting in stone what the terms of that process will be.

Before you make a meaningful commitment of any kind, always consider the worst that can happen. And if it's not acceptable, don't make the commitment.

At this point in my career, I don't do any projects that will absorb my personal time if they won't yield a million dollars in profit. A million dollars gets my attention. And for the rest of my life I don't want to do any serious deals unless they are real estate related, because I know and understand real estate. I learned through trial and error not to stray from what I know best and not to have delusions about my abilities.

Remember to make these major decisions early in the process while your values are still clear, before you become too immersed in the project to see them.

Since I sold Century 21, the way I look at investment opportunities has changed totally. For a deal to look good to me, it has to give me something more than the profit I can make by simply leaving my money in the bank. There is very little that can beat the high interest you can get on Treasury bills, with no associated risk. I can leave my money in the bank and go to Hawaii and sit under a palm tree and still make a substantial profit. So if the profit isn't higher than the interest I can get at the bank, there had better be something else in it for me. And I'm not particularly interested in more power, or more money for its own sake. My ego isn't that large and I'd rather live longer and live better than I would if I continued to knock myself out to get more of anything.

Whatever the size of the deals you are doing today, consider them small.

Your wealth will continue to grow if you think of each new venture or gain or goal achieved as only a stepping stone on the way to somewhere else. You watch for the opportunities and take advantage of them. Instead of assuming that you are setting yourself up for life in your current venture, operate on the assumption that your vision and motivation will eventually be diverted to other, bigger deals. I always felt that, other than my wife and kids, anything I had was for sale at the right price.

Inevitably, this attitude will assist you in becoming more discriminating in the type of projects you take on and the way you run them; if they seem to require a lifetime commitment of sixteen-hour days, you should either get out of them or never get into them in the first place. And do your best to make sure that things are efficiently enough run to afford you time and energy to spot other opportunities that you might wish to move on to — but only if they are bigger ones. Taking on more of the same type of venture may be counter-productive.

I was consumed by Century 21 Real Estate and I'd never take on a project like that again. I should not have taken on a similar franchise scheme like the domestic maintenance service I tried, Mr. Build, because it required the same kind of total commitment for a long period of time, and I wasn't prepared to do that anymore. Ultimately, that was one of the major considerations in declining to chase the Heritage USA purchase. And I never should have gone into some-thing like Endless Vacations, the time-sharing scheme I got involved in, because it really was a step backward to smaller deals and I was not interested in or involved in its management. Another lesson of the time-share experience was that any time you lend money to a project you run the risk of owning it later, as I did when I inherited the venture because of the bankruptcy of the borrower.

Once you've done your risk assessment and set the goals for the project, the next step is to create a business plan to map out your strategy.

The key areas to consider are structure, financing and people.

Structure
Set up your business as if bankruptcy were inevitable within ninety days and cover your assets accordingly. Consider setting up a family trust or giving half your assets to your spouse; if you go bankrupt or get

divorced, at least you will have 50 percent of what your ex-spouse has. Then you can decide which assets, if any, you are willing to jeopardize when you do a deal. If you are willing, choose specific ones and limit your obligations under any agreement to those only.

Although this may be considered heresy by some professionals, I suggest that you put each of your projects into separate limited companies. Build fire walls. Don't be so judicious about tax planning that you risk dangerous and unnecessary debt liability. Early in my career my accountants advised me to put all my projects in one company so that if any of them lost money, the losses could be written off against the others. That might have been good tax planning, since in the short term it saves money, but it was poor entrepreneurship. What the accountants failed to point out was that all the liabilities are then in one company. The bankruptcy of one project could take down the whole company. A limited company restricts liability to whatever assets are inside that company. That's why I call it building fire walls; if a fire starts to burn, it can burn only one house down. Don't let tax planning drive the company or it could drive it into the ground. Using liability planning, you can have your personal holding company at the top, then the project companies as subsidiaries, each with its own limited liability. If you lose one project, you don't lose everything.

Your companies can be subsidiaries of other companies or they can be owned by you. Give it a great deal of thought. Imagine what the worst scenario is that could happen to you before you structure the enterprise that's going to manage the deal.

If you enter into a relationship with someone else to buy a project, think about how you are going to structure that relationship. Are you going to use a new corporation? Are you going to buy into an existing company or into a limited and general partnership or a joint venture? Are you going to hold the property personally, in your own name? To deal with all these questions you need the advice of a good corporate and business lawyer. And don't hesitate to check out the background of any potential partner to determine whether he or she has a history of litigation. If prospective partners are litigious, stay away from them.

A corollary of asset protection is never grant an unlimited personal guarantee to secure any deal. When I went into business with Nelson Skalbania, I thought it was a given that if you wanted to borrow money you had to sign an unlimited guarantee; I learned the hard way that this is not so. At this stage in my career I refuse to sign a personal guarantee altogether; if my corporate value in any given venture is not good enough, then I pass on the deal. You will probably have to give some form of guarantee in order to do business — just don't ask your spouse or family or friends to sign it, and don't make it unlimited. Limit it to specific assets.

Don't neglect the structure of your personal assets, either — do estate planning early with a good lawyer and update your will annually. Select a respected mentor/adviser/business friend to act as a trustee in the event of your death and keep him or her conversant with your business enterprise. Your circumstances and fortunes will change. On your birthday, go through your will and make sure that the people you want to leave your estate to are still the same; make sure that your executors and your trustees are the people you want them to be. By reviewing your document annually you have fulfilled my definition of a living will.

Financing
To develop the financial part of your business plan, work with your advisers to develop a five-year plan for your new business. Do a cash-flow analysis for sixty individual months (or the expected life of the enterprise) with a time frame for expenditures and target dates for profits. Know exactly when you are going to have cash coming in over and above the cost of your expenditures, when income and expenditures are even and when there will be a shortfall. Once you know what your cash shortfall is going to be and for what period of time it is going to last, you will know how much money you're going to have to invest or find to make your venture happen. You plan so that the whole thing doesn't fall flat on its face because you forgot that you're going to have a payroll to meet with no money coming in. When we initially set up Century 21, we planned on six to nine months' effort before our first offices would open. Then these new offices had thirty days to make sales and then there was a delayed income-reporting structure; we had to be prepared to fund the shortfall of cash for that time.

There is an unbelievable inertia to overcome when you start up a new venture; nothing exists. There isn't a card, there isn't an address, there isn't a phone number. There isn't a pencil sharpener or a pencil. There isn't one employee. A start-up company requires someone who can get all those balls in the air and still achieve the ultimate goal: profit.

Once you have an idea of what kind of money you need, you will need to find it. When you are first starting out, use other people's money to make money. You can radically increase your net worth while still having no cash. For real estate deals, you can tie down property for as little as possible, minimize staff and do most of the work yourself. Give yourself three months to close each deal, and in the interim try to sell it for more than you will pay.

If you are using the five-year plan to take to a bank to help finance the venture, then you have to have studies of the marketplace to find out how large it is. And you have to have criteria for the people you will be working with, be they staff or potential customers. You go into the bank after assessing the market, determining its size and establishing your growth potential; then you detail how you're going to make the business a success.

Business plans are different for each company: different things have to be taken into consideration. For instance, the difficulty with a business like Century 21 was that there was nothing tangible; there would be no buildup of hard assets. I was selling my service and that's the hardest kind of business to arrange financing for. It was difficult to demonstrate to the bank in the early days before we had a track record that the brokers would in fact pay us 6 percent of their commission in return for the services we provided for them.

And one last bit of financial advice: don't supply or circulate your net worth statement — it could hang you later. Write it out carefully and have your spouse read it. Drink a glass of champagne together and then burn it. Give lenders only what they absolutely have to see in order to obtain financing.

People

As you establish the structure and consider the financing, the next question is, How are you going to accomplish all this? Who do you need in order to make this thing happen and how do you bring them on board? Who are you going to hire? All this should be spelled out in your business plan. This component — the business circle — is just as important as structure and financing.

Your business circle should include members like a trusted number two, a credible board of directors, a dynamic sales leader and marketing team, an enthusiastic office staff, a chief financial officer, a legal adviser, your banker, an R and D department and your personal support system. Be sure to fill all the positions, with no one individual, including yourself, occupying more than three positions.

Entrepreneurs have a tendency to think they know it all. If you are like me, what you really know is a little bit about a lot of things. Don't try to do everything yourself. Usually what an entrepreneur is good at is making money in the chosen business. Hire professionals to do what you can't — don't scrimp here to save money. You have to know yourself; know what your weaknesses are and where you need complementing. Beef up your skills by building a team of people. Don't hesitate to hire professional accountants or lawyers. Usually the money you put into your advisers is money well spent.

Let me give you a tip on hiring professional help: when you bring a professional onto your team, make sure his or her compensation package is negotiated up front. Otherwise you will have a heart attack when you receive your lawyer's or your accountant's bills.

Selecting your legal counsel is one of your most important strategic decisions. You must ensure that your lawyer identifies with and understands your business plan. You will be spending lots of time together solving business problems, and your legal counsel will become one of your most valued advisers. I would suggest you discuss the fee arrangement before engaging a lawyer so that you both understand and agree to it. You must not feel that you're being charged every time you make a call.

Legal cases in particular tend to take on a life of their own — they grow like Topsy in ways that are not necessarily productive. If you can hold out the promise of a lot of future business, negotiate a package deal at reduced flat rates. Decide up front what role your advisers will play and what they are going to do; stop them from working on your projects in an open-ended fashion. Be specific about the assignment and the cost.

Always remember that lawyers and accountants are just that — lawyers and accountants. They are not in business. You are the one in business and you are responsible. Don't look to your lawyers and accountants for business advice — go to someone in business.

I recall once talking to a senior partner of Touche Ross approximately five years after starting Century 21. Gary Charlwood and I asked him what he thought the future held in store for us.

Grimly he warned us that the company was just a flimsy structure built from a deck of cards, waiting to be blown over in the slightest breeze. He thought the company wasn't worth anything. We sat there stunned that he could be so naive, and told him so. But he stuck to his guns. He pointed out in his inimitable accountant's narrow way that since we had no commodities, we had no assets. According to him, all we had was a stack of contracts. He didn't understand the synergy of putting people on the balance sheet. Nevertheless, he moved up in his career to become one of the leading accountants in Canada.

When you begin to put together your board of directors, think of role models — people you admire — and look for members who emulate them. When I was selecting my first board of directors in 1968, I had just bought a book of Karsh portrait photography. I found that the black-and-white images in it were very striking. As I looked through them, the personalities of some of the people seemed to come right through the pages at me and I thought, "What a terrific group of prominent citizens of the world; wouldn't it be great to have some of these people on my board of directors?" Then I thought again: "Why can't I have them on my board?"

I looked for people who filled the roles of John Kennedy, Indira Gandhi, Martin Luther King and Ernest Hemingway first, not only to sit on my board, but also to act as mentors. I often ask myself what one of them would do in a given situation, in order to guide my endeavours. The Karsh portraits of the four hang on my office wall.

I chose Kennedy because I felt that he was a great businessman. He was aggressive, he had a charismatic personality, he was outgoing and fair-minded, and I thought he was a deal maker: he had the ability to articulate his dreams and to motivate other people to help make his dreams reality.

Indira Gandhi seemed to have a grasp of the world of tomorrow, not just what was going on today. She had a vision for the planet and she led with vision. Again, she was fair. When you're in a leadership position, it's very easy to use your position to take advantage of others. Ultimately, those who do so don't get what they want from others because they have ruined the relationship. As a business person you have to be careful that you don't do that. You have to be disciplined about it.

Any time I do a deal, I know that the deal's got to be a fair deal for the other party. It is possible to look after your own interests and at the same time make sure that the deal fits the other party's needs and that they are happy with it.

I chose Martin Luther King for all the things that he stood for. He was strong, articulate, fair, charismatic, enthusiastic and totally committed — driven. He was utterly dedicated to his goal.

Ernest Hemingway did things that other people just dream and fantasize about. I admire the things he dared to do in his life, the wide variety of experiences he had and his vision for using them creatively in his writing.

In addition to your board of directors, develop three to five mentors who are at least fifteen years your senior. They should be people you hold in highest respect. Look for people in your own field of business who have a non-competitive position. They should be people who wouldn't want to take advantage of your weaknesses. Find a mentor who is successful and who doesn't need anything you've got. If you're living in Toronto, try to get somebody in Vancouver to advise you if you are concerned about geographical competition. If you're in the franchise business, go to another franchisor selling a different product or service. Use your wits. You'll find that there are a lot of people out there who would willingly talk to you, just like Jimmy Pattison did when I needed help with Century 21.

Choose different mentors throughout your life, a minimum of one at a time, but ideally two or three, up to a maximum of five. And select them carefully according to your current needs and aspirations. They should be people you can really talk to about all aspects of your life.

When you have established your mentor group, you have to send them your hard copy — your financial statements and other essential data — and have an annual "board meeting" with them. No matter what the position on your business circle, give your key people, advisers and staff a copy of the business plan and a time frame for achieving these goals so that they can understand what you're doing and can have faith that you're going to achieve it.

Lastly, you are the most important factor in any deal or venture. Value your time like gold. Don't waste it on things that will not make you money or help you reach your goals. Constantly assess what you are doing at the moment to see if you are wasting your time. Limit the meetings you will attend and the deals you will consider in a week. Too many of either will leave you busy but unproductive, like a gerbil in an exercise wheel.

My rules for a successful business have been summarized in what I call my Seven Pillars of Entrepreneurial Wisdom.

1. *First and foremost, you have to take risks.*

   You must make sure that you have the capacity to do so. Many times, what is perceived to be risk by other people is not perceived as risk by the person who is actually taking it — the research has been done to determine the extent of the risk. Whenever you are going to venture into a new area, you have to have the stomach for risk or else you won't be successful. The ability to measure and assess risk is an essential skill.

2. *Once you settle on a market, you chase it as if your life depended on it.*

Your financial life literally depends on the area that you are going to be a player in, so you had better be fully committed to it. If you are still questioning it in your mind, you shouldn't do it. You have to be in an all-systems-go mode. Your first critical task is to develop people — staff and customers — with a positive attitude toward the venture; if you have doubts about its success, the world will, too.

3. *Leanness gives you more speed than fat and flab.*

No matter whether the economy is good or bad, you should consistently go through your corporation to see that every asset, including personnel, is essential and well utilized. You will go bankrupt if you are carrying ponderous, non-productive waste and bureaucracy. Just as cholesterol clogging the veins gathers more of the same from the bloodstream, people can clog up the arteries of your business.

Your company should be project oriented. Everyone should have a project, whether it is the accounting department or the secretaries. If they don't have a project they probably are underutilized or unnecessary. When a project ends, they had better get a new one. No one should simply be putting in their time. And all projects should have time lines and deadlines. A lean mentality is not necessarily a mean mentality — it emphasizes productivity over all else.

4. *Communication and sensitivity towards employees is the most critical part of your internal operations.*

    It is common knowledge that employees need to be part of a team. You need to show by your actions and your attitude that all your staff are essential and appreciated members of a team.

5. *Decentralization of both operations and decision making guarantees success.*

    Move your decision making down as close to the project it affects as possible. Ideally, the project manager should be the one making all the decisions.

6. *The use of new technology to increase efficiency and productivity allows you to take advantage of new opportunities.*

    If you want to fight a modern-day war, then you need modern-day weapons. From the outset, use the latest technological tools to help you compete more effectively. Don't try to do without them until some later date. Cellular phones, fax and computers are being used by your competitors. Check out your competition periodically to see if they have better tools than you do. If they do, then they probably are going to beat you. Your staff must also be trained properly to exploit new equipment to full advantage. Most importantly, with the flood of improved gizmos, you have to be sure that you really need the equipment you have and that it is the right equipment for your operation. Someone in your company must be responsible for making sure that you do not go for things because they have lots of bells and whistles or because they are fashionable.

7. *You must have a clear idea of where you are going ultimately — a strategy for the long haul.*

What's more, you must be able to express and communicate that strategy to everyone around you. Don't keep it a secret. Your staff should feel they have more than a job — they have a role to play in a long-haul strategy.

The reality is that nothing is forever so you had better learn to recognize the winds of change and have a plan ready for diversification or modification of your enterprise. Think about how long your career direction is good for and what you might do next. If you communicate well with your staff, they will let you know when they feel things changing, or feel the need for change.

THREE

How to Lose Your Shirt — And Get It Back Again: Skalbania Enterprises Limited

Prosperity is the most difficult thing in the world to handle.
> — Duke Rudman, flamboyant dandy, $200 million Texas wildcatter, and the most impressive person I have ever met.

Vancouver real estate king and quintessential venture capitalist Nelson Skalbania and I would have been in trouble even if the 1981 recession hadn't come along; all it did was salve our egos a bit, because everybody else was in trouble at the same time. Nelson and I were doing deals far too fast and not managing them at all — just buying them and literally forgetting them. After everything had fallen around us I was $30 million in debt, and my creditors wanted Century 21 Real Estate.

When Century 21 was established in British Columbia in 1976, my family moved from Edmonton to Victoria. It seemed like a great place to raise children; my wife, Donna, had given birth to two, Todd and Liane, within ten months in 1964. Before the move Donna had either worked for others or pitched in wherever necessary in my business. Most of the time visitors

67

to the office in the early days didn't even know who she was. Once, a staff member at Western Diversified in Edmonton passed the temporary receptionist on his way to see me and said, "Boy, did you see the breasts on that woman?"

"Yes," I told him. "That woman's my wife."

When we got to Victoria we lived "temporarily" in the Harbour Towers Hotel; when we separated eleven years later, it was the Harbour Towers Hotel that I moved out of in 1987. In the meantime we had renovated two suites on the top floor, where I both lived and worked. Donna used to joke that she woke up each morning to find fourteen secretaries already at work in the living room. She still just pitched right in. Over the years my business interests took over suites on the eleventh, tenth and eighth floors as well.

Most people who worked for me had no job descriptions; instead they had lists, made up by me nightly. Donna and the staff would compare them each morning. It was common to hear "What's on your list?" before they got down to work. Donna's list covered a wide range of things, including going to the store to buy six shirts; she'd bring them back, I'd choose one and she'd return the rest.

That modus operandi made it possible for me to devote all my energies to work. I was out of town so much that when Donna and the kids came to meet me at the airport she would point across the terminal toward me and announce for all to hear, "Kids, that's your father."

It didn't take long for me to cement my connection with Nelson Skalbania across the water. We'd met when I was working on a real estate project in 1972. His life in the fast lane included working hard and playing hard at a jet-set level I had only dreamed of — and in some cases, could never have imagined. Looking back on it now, I see he was living the life I thought I wanted — he was my idea of a hero and I was putty in his hands.

For some time we worked and played together on an informal basis. I'd wander into Nelson's chaotic office — it always looked as if a bomb had hit it — and find him crawling around in the mess of paper on the floor, growling hushed monosyllables at whoever was within earshot. Nelson had thirty to forty deals a day coming through his office door, and only half the ones he took on were real estate. He claimed to have a unique filing system for the projects that came his way. The best ones landed on his desk, the worst ones went immediately into the wastepaper basket and the maybes ended up on the floor. It didn't look that well organized to me.

I came by occasionally to check out the iffy stuff carpeting the office. One day in 1979 I found a prospectus for a 364-unit apartment block in Las Vegas called Cinnamon Ridge among the debris. It had eight swimming pools, terrific architecture and grounds, and a large vacancy rate. What's more, it was going cheap. I asked Nelson if he minded if I checked it out. He snapped at me not to bother him, he was busy.

Before you know it we had put together a syndicate of investors from Edmonton and, with Nelson taking a couple of units, we bought the place. My job, as it was in future deals, was to manage it so that Nelson could go right on being busy.

We did everything in the book to attract tenants to Cinnamon Ridge. We sent out letters to all the casinos promising them a good rate for their visiting acts; we gave away appliances to new tenants and bonuses to existing tenants who brought in new people. But we didn't make much progress reducing the vacancy rate — not until the Club Lido girls arrived from Paris.

One of the casinos eventually took us up on our offer and sent us the entire revue of gorgeous French women from the Lido for the duration of their stay. The first thing they did was take off their bikini tops and lounge around the pools. An irate tenant called the police, and soon the press was everywhere. The headline in the paper the next day read: Naked Lido Girls at Cinnamon Ridge.

The entire project was immediately and forever 100 percent booked. Three years later we made $2 million on the building when we sold it.

It wasn't only business that we did at Las Vegas: Nelson loved to gamble, and so did the high-flying wheeler-dealers he knew. On special occasions we'd hop on his private jet — and this was no pint-sized Lear, this was the grown-up kind — and take off to Las Vegas for the weekend. On the way down, Nelson would flip through various deals he was considering and then get someone to play backgammon with him for the rest of the trip. Limos would meet us at the airport and whisk us off to Caesar's Palace, where Nelson was granted special status because he was such a good customer.

I loved the shows and dinners and parties. Gambling didn't interest me but I loved to watch it in action. The amount of money Nelson and his friends lost in less than half an hour I'm sure more than equalled the GNP of some small nations. Once when Nelson went to the washroom, he came back fifteen minutes later to find that he had lost several thousand dollars. But it meant nothing to him; he just kept right on playing without batting an eye. A friend of his once sat down to dinner, placed his pre-dinner drink order and went off to do some gambling until it arrived; when he came back ten minutes later he had lost $50,000. By Monday morning we were all back at work, earning the money to do the same thing all over again.

On one such trip we continued on to La Jolla, California, where Caesar's Palace kept a private home for its prize clientele. It had a full complement of staff and seven bedrooms, each with its own private bathroom the size of most people's houses. Everything was laid on.

I was tired from all the late nights and literally passed out on arrival. By midnight I was wide awake again, so Nelson and I went for a twenty-mile run to the ocean and back. We galloped for hours like wild horses through the fields and along the beach, racing the wind in the moonlight. We returned at four in the morning exhilarated and ready to take on the world.

I was hooked. These were the guys I wanted to play with and this was the lifestyle I wanted.

We started buying property together at a tremendous velocity in 1979 with the formation of our corporation, Skalbania Enterprises Limited. It went public in 1980 when we bought 80 percent of a shell company listed on the Vancouver Stock Exchange with about $1 million each and some property. We decided to go public to raise money quickly in order to buy more product, as well as for tax-credit considerations. I was to be the property manager and resale broker, which entitled me to a commission.

The wheeling and dealing gave me an adrenaline high. I had been doing million-dollar deals and later $10-million deals on my own before that time, but Nelson was the biggest, fastest, most convincing operator there was — his deals were $100-million deals, and I jumped on the bandwagon.

In his pithy and irreverent style, Nelson called what we did the Five Easy Steps of Real Estate Development:

1. No money.
2. No brains.
3. No education.
4. Buy low.
5. Sell high.

Nelson had the charisma and the connections to get the deals, and I had the stable cash flow to support them in Century 21, as well as proven property-development and management skills. We thought we were a perfect match. Even after Nelson ran out of money, people were still advancing him money on crazy schemes for a long time because of his powerful personality. No one consulted lawyers about deals then. The real estate market was so hot in 1980 that everyone just dove in. But most people thought about it a little longer than Nelson, who grabbed everything in sight while other folks were mulling deals over. Nelson says that I'm the quickest yes-no man he has ever met; my immediate reaction to a deal was almost always yes, but if I had a chance to sleep on it overnight the answer inevitably changed to no. So he made a practice of getting me to sign on the dotted line before I went to bed.

After we formed our company we went about acquiring lines of credit from banks, starting with the Royal Bank at $5 million. We used that money to locate properties to invest in; it didn't take us three months to go through that $5 million. We went on a shopping spree, jetting all over North America. All the lending institutions were throwing money at us. They were sold by Nelson and eager to exploit the booming real estate market. In every case they were as much at fault as the players were. They jumped right on the bandwagon, just like I did.

I was so grateful to Nelson Skalbania for bringing me into his world that one day when I was in a generous mood I bought him an antique penny-farthing bicycle, which decorated his office thereafter. He claims that it is the best gift I ever gave him. But it was nothing compared to his gift to me: my first taste of the jet-set life.

Once, we hopped on the DeHavilland DH-125 Nelson had just bought from department-store magnate Chunky Woodward and headed for Salt Lake City. The plane sat eight people and was like travelling around in a living room; over the years, a lot of business was done on that airplane. At Salt Lake City Nelson offered $25 million in cash for a property we looked at there. Much to my relief they turned him down — we didn't have $25 million in cash. When I asked Nelson incredulously what he would have done if they had said yes, he just brushed me off with, "I'd think of something."

The next stop was San Diego, where we offered $30 million cash for a beautiful condominium development. This time the vendors bit. Nelson flipped it to Vancouver developer Jeffrey Lau within thirty days.

When Nelson first got the plane he was a bit of a greenhorn at the jet-set life — he didn't know that when you owned the plane you could tell the pilot where to fly. On the way home from one trip, I reminded him that I lived in Victoria and asked if he could drop me there. With a befuddled look he said he'd have to ask the pilot. He strode up to the cockpit and came back with a big grin on his face. "Sure." He beamed, "We can take you there!"

We arrived at Victoria airport in the middle of the night with our landing lights off. The police were waiting there to greet us — they wanted to know what sort of unidentified flying object had dropped out of the sky in the wee hours of the morning. Luckily I happened to know the policemen, so after I had reassured them that all was well, they gave me a ride home.

Another time I told Nelson that I was going to Edmonton to do some business with David Cowley of Cowley-Keith Real Estate. Nelson said that he was going there too, and offered me a ride on his plane. When we got there we went our separate ways and met again at the airport for the return flight.

On the way back I asked Nelson if he had bought anything, and he said no. He asked if I had, and I told him about a terrific $1 million office building that I had just put $5,000 down on. I made it sound so good that Nelson wanted a piece of the action.

"Don't you think I should be in on this too?" he asked. "Shouldn't we go fifty-fifty?"

I thought that was a great idea, so I asked him for a $2,500 cheque. He wrote it on the spot.

I flipped the building within two weeks, before the sale was closed, and made $25,000 — half of which was Nelson's. At $12,500, that made the round trip from Vancouver to Edmonton the most expensive plane ride in the world.

The single most important principle between Nelson and me was that our word was our bond. One time when we were both in Edmonton on business we met in a squash club on the way back to the airport. We sat for twenty minutes high in the bleachers, scribbling one $5.6 million deal and one $6.3 million deal on the back of two drink coasters. Waiting at the bottom were my Victoria lawyer, David Adams, and Nelson's wife, Eleni, famous for her superb Vancouver hotel, The Wedgewood. When we climbed down from the bleachers I handed the coasters to David and asked him to write the deals up.

He just looked at me incredulously. When he recovered he warned me in stern tones that I had to document my transactions more carefully. He didn't understand then, although he learned quickly, that trust was the standard method of operation between Nelson and me, and always would be. Once he got used to that — and the fact that I would not infrequently call him at four in the morning for advice — he handled all my business transactions until I moved to Vancouver. I offered to hire him full-time, but after he thought about it for a while he declined; he said that as long as he was self-employed he still had the option of telling me to get lost.

My present CEO at Samoth Capital, Eugene Kaulius, a chartered accountant with a banking background, was also at the time looking after Eleni Skalbania's business affairs. It was no secret that Eugene's main task was to keep Nelson at arm's length from Eleni's money. One day when Eugene and Eleni were about to leave for Victoria to check out a potential investment, Nelson emerged from his office looking disgruntled.

"You know," he moaned, "if Edgar Kaiser wants to talk to Eleni, Eleni goes running. If Jack Poole wants to talk to Eleni, Eleni goes running. But if Nelson Skalbania wants to talk business with Eleni, he's told to speak to Eugene Kaulius."

In the fall of 1981, the lights went out.

One day brokers filled the offices of Skalbania Enterprises on Cardero Street, desperate to do business with us. At any one time you could count ten or fifteen people milling about in the lobby, waiting their turn.

The next day the place was empty. The only people who showed up after that were desperate brokers trying to unload their own shaky deals on us.

We had purchased property that we thought we could resell quickly, and found that prospective purchasers were not closing — in spite of putting deposits down. Skalbania Enterprises was left with huge tracts of property and no place to sell it. Most of it was development property, so there was very little cash flow.

What happened was that interest rates had soared to a prime of 24 percent and the ten largest real estate companies in North America — all of which were Canadian — simply stopped buying. Daon, Nuwest, Carma — no one would put up the money, and mortgaged assets remained unsold. In Alberta, the value of some properties declined to 10 percent of their former worth within two months. The properties weren't worth the value of the down payment, never mind the mortgage. In that province values have never returned to the pre-1981 level; in British Columbia they did, but not until 1990.

But the root of the problem was a classic case of the King Arthur Syndrome. Nelson and I thought we were invincible. In the first flush of magnificent, repeated success, many entrepreneurs go under because they believe they can do no wrong. They take no advice and accept none. They don't do their homework. They are

My mother, Trude, and I lived in England where she worked as a nanny to the Haig family until we came to Canada in 1945.

I joined the army when I was fifteen. In 1959, I served in the Suez Canal region, patrolling the armistice demarcation line between Egypt and Israel when I wasn't cutting a deal with the Bedouins.

When I joined First Investors Corporation I was a sales manager trainee under the watchful eye of my manager, Ken Marlin (right).

1967

Regular bonuses, seminars and company dinners kept staff at First Investors and sister companies in the Principal Group motivated. Here Donald Cormie (left) presides over a table of sales staff and families.

Despite the Principal Group's failings, the marketing and motivational strategies were impressive. This cartoon and poem appeared in the company's newsletter "The Crusader". Every month top sales staff were honoured company-wide.

Courtesy of K. Marlin

OL' KING THOMAS

PETE'S HARD TO BEAT!

How come so much honour goes—
Not to all the Jacks and Joes?
When campaigns start they jes' can't beat
That Ol' King Thomas, known as Pete!

He took the Dishwasher and a Clock—
(When's the fella gonna stop?)
Now he's touted "King of the Ball"
His sales in March have topped 'em all!

When I first heard about Art Bartlett (left), his partner Marsh Fischer (right) and Century 21 in 1974, the franchise seemed like a crazy scheme. But the more I listened, the better it sounded.

Gary Charlwood (below) and I finally ended our Century 21 partnership in 1989. The headlines said "Thomas Gunned Down" but at the end of the day I put $23 million in the bank.

Nelson Skalbania (above) had a unique filing system for proposals: the best landed on his desk, the worst went into the wastebasket and the maybes ended up on the floor. I came by regularly to check out the iffy stuff on the carpet and soon became a partner in both the deals and the high life.

When I realized I was $30 million in debt, I hired John Norton to be my corporate bail-out lawyer. Since our successful battle to stave off bankruptcy, we've gone on to more enjoyable pursuits.

What if they held an auction and nobody bid? Lawyer Paul Misch (right) joined me at Heritage Properties. This was when everyone wanted a piece of the action.

Eugene Kaulius (far right), Ken Marlin (third from right) and I posed with members of the PTL organization. This was before we withdrew our offer.

To motivate staff I always plan surprises in addition to the regular incentives and bonuses. One day I closed the office and took them all out to a speedway where they did a high performance driving course.

Since I sold Century 21, I have taken more time to enjoy life. I've gone skydiving, flown helicopters, driven a Formula One race car . . .

Courtesy of P. Thomas

and gone up in a hot air balloon.

At the height of my financial crisis in 1982, I began calling in some loans of my own. One repayment was a management contract for a singing group called The Nylons instead of cash. The investment in The Nylons (l to r: Arnold Robinson, Claude Morrison, Micah Barnes and Billy Newton-Davis) has been a long term one and a lot of fun.

Denise Grant

overtaken with ambition, ego and greed, and so were we.

The running joke around my office at the time was that the only reason the debt wasn't $50 million or $100 million was that I didn't go over to Vancouver more often. I was living in Victoria, and I would drop by Nelson's Vancouver office weekly to check out the deals he had signed up; I'd sign on the dotted line whenever a guarantor was required. I signed unlimited personal guarantees and became what is known as a "joint debtor." But I didn't understand what the words "joint and several" in the loan documents really meant. Those words made me responsible for 100 percent of the guarantees that we had signed together, if Nelson couldn't pay.

Our problems were mind-boggling, and we didn't think we were so smart anymore. We didn't realize that when you sign a mortgage guarantee, you buy a piece of property — an apartment building, say — and you are the owner until that mortgage is torn up. You might put a million dollars down and sign a $5 million mortgage. If someone else comes along eventually and offers a significantly higher price for that building, you take it and the buyer assumes the mortgage. You put your money in the bank and forget about that building.

Three years later someone from a bank may knock on your door and say, "The apartment block isn't worth what the mortgage is and the owner can't pay; I want my mortgage money back."

You would probably insist that you are not involved in that apartment block because you sold it three years ago. But the problem is that your guarantee is still on the mortgage: You owe the money!

Problems like that affected not only Skalbania

Enterprises, but also the many other properties I owned or had owned independently. In one case I had built an apartment block in Port Hardy, B.C., for about a million dollars in construction costs; a syndicate in Vancouver bought it for $1.5 million, and they in turn sold it for $2.2 million to a group of doctors. Three years later the bank called me on my original guarantee, which was about $800,000. All the rest of the investors had lost everything, and the building wasn't worth any more than the mortgage I had originally signed. Today it is once again worth more than a million dollars.

In 1984 Nelson Skalbania provided *Canadian Business* with a perfect anecdote to describe the tenor of those crisis days. In it the two of us are huddled in a typical emergency meeting, trying to save our bacon. On this particular occasion we were struggling to keep the Royal Bank from hauling us into court. When we quit for the day, we decided to go for a run in Stanley Park:

> We're about two miles into the park when, all of a sudden, out of the bushes comes a guy fully dressed — suit, street shoes, hat, the whole thing — running along beside me. He says to me, "Hi, Nelson, mind if I jog along?" I say, "Sure, go ahead," and he puffs along for maybe a quarter of a mile and finally asks, "You know Peter Thomas?"
>
> Now, I've had some things happen to me in my time and I'm getting suspicious. I say, "Yeah, I've heard of him, why?" The guy says, "Oh, nothing. I heard he was out for a jog with you." I say, "Nope, haven't seen him," and introduce Peter as John So-and-So. You could see the guy clomping

along in his suit thinking: "How do I get out of this one?" Eventually we just picked up our pace and left him in the middle of the park. The next day, I found out that the guy was trying to serve a subpoena that would have had us in court. The bank was as mad as hell that they'd missed Peter.

By mid-1982, creditors were harassing us at every turn. At one point we had seventeen summonses in one day, and my wife was looking for a place to hide the family silver. We were in so much trouble that I was being hassled constantly and couldn't get any work done.

Amazingly enough, the Victoria community was very protective of my family. We had been there for six years and were well liked, and those who had to do the dirty work didn't like doing it. A process server in town at the time used to call to see if I was home before he showed up with his summons; it was a warning to stay out of sight. He'd say to Donna, "Peter isn't home now, is he? He's out of town?" And then he'd show up at the hotel suite door. I learned to take the stairs rather than the elevator, all twelve flights.

One night when Donna and I were at dinner in a local restaurant I noticed someone sitting across the room watching us all evening. When the meal was nearly over I got up, approached the gentleman and asked him if he was waiting for me. He said that yes, he was, and handed me a summons. "I didn't want to interrupt your dinner, sir."

In November 1982 we just got out of town. We headed for Puerto Vallarta in Mexico, where we had planned to go on vacation before things started to heat up the previous summer.

After we got back I decided to go to Texas to try to make some cash flow, since there was none passing through Vancouver. I'd been invited to do some speaking there, and arranged with Gary Charlwood to investigate the possibility of selling a Uniglobe regional franchise, which would have earned me a tidy $100,000 commission. I drove down to Texas alone to give myself some time to cool out. Donna was to fly down and meet me there.

When I got to Texas I talked to Nelson by phone and discovered that the situation was getting more and more desperate. But he promised that he wouldn't do anything drastic until I got back. I was at the Mansion Hotel in Dallas, where I was about to give a speech to the Young Presidents' Organization. I promised Nelson that I would get back home as soon as possible after that.

Two days later, on Wednesday, December 8, 1982, while Donna and I were driving home, I called in to the office for messages and found that there was one from friend and fellow Century 21 director David Radler. When I called him back, what he had to tell me changed my life irrevocably.

The night before, David had been to a dinner of sausages and sauerkraut with 450 other people at Vancouver's posh Bayshore Hotel, famous for putting up Howard Hughes. The dinner was thrown by Nelson Skalbania, and many of the guests were his creditors. After dinner Nelson had announced that he was "restructuring his debt." He owed his creditors nearly $40 million, and he couldn't pay.

According to a Southam News story run on December 9, Nelson had announced that "the income-tax collectors, in their wisdom, have made it impossible for me to function. I'd like to earn some dollars to pay my creditors, but I can't with that terrible albatross over my head. . . . I have to free myself from all the shackles that are draped over my skinny shoulders so that I can finally start fresh with my wife." The article continued:

Tearfully, he made three pledges to his estranged wife:

First, to get out from under his debts.

Second, that this Tuesday-night statement would be "the last god-damned appearance of Skalbania before the media."

And third, that he would, in future, be the "damnedest, most loving, and considerate husband possible."

Skalbania apologized to his guests — including multimillionaire and would-be Tory leader Peter Pocklington, who sat at his side — if what he had to say was embarrassing to them.

It was the death of a deal-junkie. In the media blitz that followed the bizarre dinner and Nelson's stunning announcement, the name of Peter Thomas was never mentioned once.

Much to the surprise of many people, my reaction to the announcement, after the initial shock wore off, was primarily one of relief. Sure I was scared — like a drowning person I saw my whole life passing before my eyes. It made me think that everything I had ever done was a mistake, if it all was going to lead up to this: losing everything.

But I discovered that people in dire financial straits, struggling to stay afloat, feel rescued when finally forced to confess to the world that the jig is up. I might not have admitted it to myself, but I knew it was going to happen eventually. Finally, the torture was over. Now I could make a fresh start and get on with cleaning up the mess. I was glad to end the struggle.

People also are surprised that I don't feel betrayed by Nelson's failure to notify me, but it's true. First of all, I was only a small part of Nelson's empire — he did less than 25 percent of his real estate deals with me — and this venture wasn't the only one that was going down. The 1981 recession had cost him $50 million the previous year — $12 million on sports ventures alone (the Montreal Alouettes, the Calgary Boomers soccer team and the Vancouver Canadians baseball team) — and $32 million of that was in cash. The federal government was claiming $4.4 million dollars in back taxes. His protracted and difficult divorce settlement with his high-school sweetheart was costing him $30,000 a month for the cash settlement alone. On top of that, his second wife, Eleni, had left him two weeks before. In retrospect, Skalbania Enterprises was probably the least of his worries.

Knowing Nelson the way I do, I'm sure that what he did was an impulsive act. What few people know is that between the time of our phone conversation and the time of his dinner, he had escorted around town a group of Hong Kong investors whom he had been trying to lure to Vancouver for some time. Their arrival was his big chance to unload some property and perhaps remain solvent.

As he was showing these gentlemen around in his white Rolls-Royce Corniche, he stopped at a red light. A car pulled up next to him and the driver leaned out the window.

"Are you Nelson Skalbania?" the driver asked.

"Yes," answered Nelson.

The next thing he knew, a summons flew through the car window and landed in his lap.

It was the last straw.

The first thing the trustees took was the penny-farthing bike.

While in Texas I had talked to Gary Charlwood from time to time regarding the sale of the Uniglobe regional franchise. Just as Donna and I were leaving for the drive back to Vancouver, we spoke again and Gary indicated that he had a very interesting proposition for me and would like to talk to me about it. We arranged to meet in Las Vegas en route home.

Gary flew to Las Vegas and showed up at our place with Len Pye of Touche Ross, Century 21's auditor, in tow. Expressing great sympathy for my financial difficulties, Gary announced that he was there to help me resolve them.

In about ten minutes he outlined a plan to bail me out in my hour of need by paying me $10,000 a month for ten years in any tax location of my choice in exchange for my 72 percent interest in Century 21 Real Estate. He hauled out elaborate pro formas demonstrating just how bad business at Century 21 was and how wonderful it was for him to be my saviour. My wife excused herself, went to the washroom and threw up.

Although most people had no idea how closely connected I was to Nelson Skalbania, Gary Charlwood had inside information and knew how vulnerable I was. He had put two and two together overnight and decided to take immediate action.

I told him no, thank you.

Between Skalbania Enterprises and my independent projects, I was sitting on $30 million in debt. After Nelson's little dinner, his creditors' eyes turned toward Peter Thomas. It didn't take long for them to fix their gaze on Century 21 Real Estate.

It was time to go into a war footing. We were going to have a war for sure, because no matter how much Century 21 was earning at that point, there wasn't enough money to look after everybody immediately — and everybody wanted to be paid immediately.

I knew I was in deep trouble, so I asked around for the best corporate bail-out lawyer in British Columbia to handle my battle with the creditors. Many people recommended Norton Stewart and Company, and I talked to John Norton there. His expertise filled the bill.

I dug out my old helmet from my army years. It was covered with camouflage fabric and decorated with bits of scrub brush. I put it into a cab and sent it over to the offices of John Norton and he swung into action.

Even before I had to deal with the Skalbania Enterprises crisis I had done battle with bankers and accountants. Like anyone with a growing company, when I first went into business for myself and again in the first years of Century 21 Real Estate Canada, we always had cash-flow problems. In the end it meant sweating the payroll. On a given payday, we'd sit with the bankers and auditors and they'd say things like, "You recall that the last time we chatted here, we told you you'd have to have an inventory turnover of 8.3 times and you're only achieving 7.8 times and so the result is that over a period of years..." I'd be sitting there thinking, "If I don't give my cheques to my employees in twenty minutes, I'll lose fifty good people and the whole thing will come crashing down. And he's talking to me about 7.8 versus 8.3?"

Several times in my career of building corporations from scratch, there has not been enough money to pay the overhead. I recall many times when I and the senior executives could not afford to draw salaries. Many times we would forfeit our pay in order to keep the corporation going.

And we always made the payroll, one way or another. If you are an entrepreneur, you simply find creative ways to do it every time. You buy some time — a week would be like a gift from God — and you run around until you get the money. When you are finished covering the payroll, then you have to hustle to pay the contractors or the suppliers or whatever — it never ends. It happens to everybody, so don't feel like a failure when it happens to you.

In 1980 I borrowed $5 million collateralized by several projects that, by 1983, after the 1982 recession, were worth considerably less than the outstanding debt against them and the lenders decided that they wanted their money back immediately. I sat down with my accountant and lawyer and the loan manager to see if we could work out a repayment schedule that would keep all of us happy. After some time the manager and I came to an agreement whereby I would pay back $200,000 a year for eleven years. Monthly instalments came to $16,666. With great relief, we all went home.

As you can see, we had arrived at a lesser amount than I actually owed, but it was not in the lenders' best interest to bankrupt me, because then they would not have received any money. The only asset they had that was worth anything was my personal guarantee, so it was in their best interest to allow me to pay what I could afford.

I immediately went back to the office and drafted a letter confirming our agreement and attached a cheque to it for the first instalment. Off it went to the bank.

The following week I got a call from a man with a thick Scottish brogue who introduced himself as the new bank manager. He told me that the last one had been fired, and he wanted to see me immediately.

I walked into the manager's office with some trepidation. As soon as I sat down, without a word he handed me a letter stating that all agreements made by the previous manager were null and void. It went on to say that what the bank required from me was a $2.5 million down payment and $500,000 per year on my $5 million loan or they would proceed with bankruptcy action.

I read the letter. Before I could say anything the Scotsman said, "Now, don't ya try any o' yer fancy salesman's stuff on me."

I just looked at him, the blood draining from my face. He wasn't finished. "Now tell me, sir, what're ya goin' ta doo aboot it?"

I could barely get my jaw to move or my voice box to emit the sound of the words: "I think I'm going to vomit on your desk."

He wanted my answer immediately, but I insisted on going back to my office to think about it. As soon as possible I sat down with my lawyers to plan a course of action. Their advice was that the bank was dead in the water if they had cashed that first cheque. They had.

The next day I called and told the Scotsman that he had no right to back out of the deal. The dispute never went to court and the settlement stuck.

Whenever you find yourself sitting opposite a depressing banker or lawyer, try this visualization exercise. Think about moments in your life that have given you great joy — you'll find that it will be hard for them to break down your morale when you do. When I was going through my 1982 crisis and found myself dealing constantly with lawyers and bankers, I used to think of a favourite picnic setting I used to go to with my wife and kids when the children were young. You can always eventually turn around a nasty lawyer or banker with your enthusiasm and positive attitude. Or, as Harry Truman noted on a sign on his desk *Nil illegitimi carborundum:* Don't let the bastards grind you down.

BATTLE PLAN FOR A BANKRUPTCY WAR

Make sure your lawyers have enough money from the very first day so that they can look after you to the bitter end.

Financial institutions have a bottomless pit of money to fight you, and that is how they usually win. You've got to put your lawyer in a position to go to the creditors and say, "Look, I've been instructed, I've got the money in trust to cover my fees, so I'll fight you to the end. You can't bleed my client to death with legal fees because I have a large war chest." If you don't have a nest egg like Century 21, sell off some assets. Better yet, set up an emergency fund at the outset for just such a crisis.

What I did was cash in my RRSP, pay the tax due and give the balance of the proceeds (approximately $200,000) to my lawyer to fight the upcoming legal war.

Don't roll over and play dead.

Don't turn over all your assets and say, "Here, take all of it, do with it as you please." It is crucial to begin negotiations by saying, "Look, if I turn it all over, it won't satisfy everybody anyway. So let's sit down and see how we can work things out." This is easier to do the more creditors you have, because then you can divide and conquer; if I had had only one creditor, that strategy would not have worked. This concept is just an extension of the old adage that says that if you owe a little money, you are in trouble; if you owe a lot of money, the lender is in trouble. The more lenders you have in trouble, the more likely they will cooperate to avoid being the one that is left out in the cold.

With the major lenders you do your best to act like a nice guy — until they turn you over to the heavyweights in what is euphemistically called the "realization department." Count on the small creditors — including the smaller banks — to stick around to the bitter end. A printer to whom you owe $5,000 is going to need his money a lot more than a bank will their $1 million; if all your creditors are like the printer, you are in much more trouble than you would be if you were dealing with financial institutions. You should always try to look after the small creditors as soon as possible — they are the ones most likely to force you into bankruptcy.

The person who made sure I didn't roll over and play dead was Eugene Kaulius, who kept all the big boys at bay. This tall, soft-spoken, sweet-looking guy crept like a cat through a terrifying mine field of debt. I had done business with him when he worked for a credit union in Victoria and I knew that in 1983 he was working for a wealthy Victoria family. I was travelling in the States a lot because the heat was so bad in Canada, and I needed someone to look after my interests at home — someone who could get me out of the mess I was in. So I called Eugene and offered to bring him and his wife to Las Vegas for a weekend to discuss the challenge of a lifetime. He made the trip, but when he heard me out, at first he said no to the deal. I had to come back with perhaps the toughest sales pitch I have ever had to make to get him to come on board. There were promises of great things for him in the future if he got me out of the jam I was in and finally he bit. He worked for me part-time at first, as well as for Eleni Skalbania and the Victoria family. When the dust settled and I was on my feet again, he joined Samoth Capital full-time.

Eugene's style is reflected in this calligraphic inscription on his office wall, spoken originally by U.S. President Calvin Coolidge:

Press on. Nothing in the world can take the place of persistence. Talent will not; nothing is more common than unsuccessful men with talent. Genius will not; unrewarded genius is almost a proverb. Education alone will not; the world is full of educated derelicts. Persistence and determination alone are omnipotent.

The Royal Bank in particular required Eugene's persistence. They were ready to force me into bankruptcy immediately. We kept trying to negotiate a settlement, but we weren't getting to the right person at bank headquarters in Montreal. We were getting no action at all. Finally I went to Montreal and found the man in the "intensive care unit" — as bankers call the department that deals with people in my predicament — who was willing and able to deal with us. Then I called Eugene and told him to get on the next plane.

When he arrived I was in the middle of reviewing my assets, one at a time, with the bank official. I was trying desperately to convince him that I was going to be able to produce the required revenue. I was in my selling mode.

Each time the banker said, "Look at this project: there's no cash flow — there will be no profit in the foreseeable future," I'd reassure him that things were going to be whipped into shape, given enough time. We were going to do all kinds of wonderful things, and the project was going to be wildly profitable very soon. Everything was going to be great. Then we'd pay off every penny we owed.

Eugene just sat there getting paler and paler. Finally he called me out of the room.

"Peter," he said with a pained look on his face, "do you want to be paying off the Royal Bank for the rest of your life? Do you want your grandchildren to be paying it off?"

I thought that that was not a good idea.

"Then stop making promises and go home. Leave it to me."

I did. Eugene achieved a negotiated settlement for repayment of the debt. It included an agreement on a percentage of the dollar value of the debt and a realistic payment structure.

The bank that held the Century 21 Real Estate account, Toronto Dominion, was on the verge of dipping directly into it to get the Skalbania Enterprises' line of credit back. Not only did they know exactly what was in the till, they knew that we had deposited my last quarterly shareholder's cheque in another bank.

When Eugene was confronted about it, his knees went weak. He was not prepared. He collected himself and finally launched into an impassioned speech about all the money that these lawsuits were costing us. It went something like this:

> How do you expect us to pay for those lawsuits? If it weren't for creditors forcing us into legal action, we could pay off our debts! It's you guys who are wasting our time so that we can't get back to work and generate income.
>
> What would you have done if we had deposited the cheque in Peter Thomas's regular account? Why, you'd have grabbed it, that's what! And then where would we be? So we went to the closest bank to our office, one where no one knew us and none of you guys would think of looking, and opened an account and stuck it in there. So there!

It worked.

Buy time. When you are finished doing that, buy more time.

Again, it was Eugene who simply stared the banks down in his own quiet, gentle, devastatingly successful way. When he could buy no more time and I had to actually show up for a meeting to discharge the debt, then I swung into action.

When we were trying to settle with the B.C. Central Credit Union, to whom Skalbania Enterprises owed $4 million, it took about six months for the lawyers to agree to a meeting and to the terms of that meeting. Of course, time was ticking away, and I was hoping for it to continue ticking. The more time went by, the more likely it was that we would come out of the recession and I'd be solvent again.

When we finally arrived at this meeting, my staff and lawyers faced off with the credit union's team: they had a whole battery of lawyers there. The first thing that happened was that their team's manager looked me in the eye and said, "Well, did you bring the money?"

I sat back. "If this is the way things are going to start," I began, "there is no point in having the meeting. Not if we are just going to insult each other. I came here to try to work out a way to pay you back. If we can do that, great. If we are going to sit here and insult each other, I'm not interested in staying."

The lawyers continued with preliminary comments. After a few minutes, the opposition's manager looked at me again and said, "Does that mean you didn't bring the money?"

I walked out. The lawyers just looked at each other. Finally my team followed me out the door. It took another two months to get a meeting. I had bought more time.

Assess each liability individually.

In many cases, the guarantees I signed for loans that had been called were not valid, for a variety of legal reasons. For instance, some of them were not executed properly — they'd been added on as an afterthought after the money changed hands. In order to have a binding guarantee, you must get something in exchange for it. Signing a guarantee months after a loan has been advanced can void the guarantee.

In some cases, people thought that there were guarantees, but when the records were examined there were none — that's how fast Nelson was playing, and the banks went along with it. If you look at banking forms and procedures today, you'll find that that could never happen now — operations have been tightened up considerably and forms have changed.

But the most interesting aspect of the case of the disappearing guarantees was a technicality that my lawyer John Norton's partner, Sandy Angus, came up with. He argued that all of the Canadian banks' variable-prime-rate promissory notes were unenforceable, and therefore so were their guarantees. The guarantees were unenforceable because the amount outstanding in each case was uncertain; you couldn't enforce an agreement with an uncertain amount attached to it. And the amount was uncertain because it was based on the prime rate — the absolute minimum rate offered to only the very best clients, like governments and large corporations. Sandy demonstrated that there was no one prime rate, because the bank had lent money at rates below what it called "prime." He discovered that the chartered bank in question had lent money to the Canadian Wheat Board below their declared prime — so in effect there was no prime. Poof go the guarantees.

Lead the creditors through the fine points of your case slowly over time. Never tell them what to think — they have their own legal counsel.

Quietly point out the relevant clauses and possible legal ramifications and let the creditors draw their own conclusions. If they are smart, they will conclude that it will be extremely difficult, time-consuming and expensive to deal with these fine points in court.

The pièce de résistance — the final legal ramification pointed out to the creditors in my case months after negotiations began — was this: my contract with Century 21 International for the Canadian franchise territory included a bankruptcy clause that provided for the territory to revert to them in the event of bankruptcy.

I discovered this because I cast around for advice and assistance, asking several people how I could protect Century 21. It was my golden egg — I had to find out if there was a way to keep the creditors from getting to it.

John Norton discovered that there was. Under the terms of the bankruptcy clause in the original franchise agreement, the creditors would get nothing if they pushed too far.

I flew down to International headquarters in Irvine, California, with Peter Podvinikov, head of the B.C. Central Credit Union, one of my largest creditors. He thought he could get around this clause by going directly to International and getting them to consent to an assignment or waiver of this right of reversion. We met with Dick Laughlin, president of International, to see if he was willing to consider assigning or waiving this right. To my great relief, Dick assured Peter that they were fully prepared to enforce their rights through Canadian courts if necessary. What he actually said was that he was "rigidly inflexible" on the issue.

That wasn't all. My lawyers suggested to the creditors' lawyers later that, since I had maintained an excellent relationship with Century 21 International, when the rights reverted to them they might possibly return them to the best man for the job — the guy who had built the company up from ground zero and made it fly: Peter Thomas, after his bankruptcy was discharged.

Again, this was all a matter of possibilities suggested by one lawyer to another. They knew from the beginning that in the event of my bankruptcy, Century 21 was worth nothing as an asset. My lawyers had already fended off creditors anxious to take control of Century 21 many times with the argument that I had developed the best team to look after it — my record with Century 21 itself was impeccable. So why bring in someone else? It followed logically to suggest that Century 21 International might feel the same way.

Right or not, all of these quibbles would only get the creditors deeper into a financial hole, should they go to court. The bankruptcy clause turned Century 21 into a golden egg with a glass cage around it. There was a sign on the glass cage that read: *If you break the glass, the gold will disappear.*

I'm not for a minute suggesting that you should have such a bankruptcy clause in your agreements — you should do your best to get it removed. Just make sure you don't make the mistakes that I made that cost me $30 million.

In retrospect, the financial cost of those mistakes pales in comparison to the personal cost. It required a great deal of self-discipline and imagination to ensure that I did not self-destruct during this experience.

The danger to beware of is the temptation to work hard and play hard. After a few years of this sort of life in Edmonton, I was drinking too much, staying awake too long and not getting enough rest, smoking and gaining weight. I knew that wasn't the right way to be dealing with stress but it took me a long time to do something about it. In 1973 I started a serious program of running, long before it became popular in my area.

My associates thought that it was pretty funny, but I ignored them.

The crunch finally came years later when Nelson Skalbania undertook his corporate restructuring. I knew what my weaknesses were, having been through a crisis before, and I knew that I was about to give in to them. There were hard lessons to be learned and decisions to be made. Mine were as follows:

Try to recognize the fact that you are in trouble as early as possible, so that you do not lose your decision-making ability and find yourself at the mercy of the banks and/or receivers who will make decisions in their favour, not necessarily in yours. Don't be afraid to talk to your peers and your friends about your problem because you are not unique in it; there is nothing to be ashamed of and perhaps they can advise and assist you. Most bankruptcies occur because the entrepreneurs did not seek help quickly enough. By the time it was obvious that they needed help, it was too late.

When I went to Australia in 1989 to check out the possibility of acquiring the Australian rights to Century 21, I discovered that the regional franchise had got into grave financial problems. The owners of the territory, Max and Brian Taylor, had run up approximately $9 million in debt building up the operation. The banks that had lent them the money were getting anxious because there was little revenue. They wound up pulling the plug and putting Max and Brian out of business. Had the owners talked to me about my experience, I would have told them that the first signs that they were in trouble occurred when they had gone through $2 million and that they should have stopped pumping money into the operation then. They should have been able to make the enterprise float without that kind of leverage. We built the Canadian territory with no bank debt at all. International took the Australian franchise back and ran it and the two men were left with $9 million in debts. They lost all their other assets to pay off that debt.

Maintain your personal agenda in times of strife. If your normal agenda is to go to a movie on a Saturday night, go to the movie on Saturday night. Go through the motions of living a normal life. When one part of your life is in chaos, the more stable and routine the rest of your life can be, the better. Continue going to work and keeping regular office hours — don't let your schedule become erratic. Then things will get back on track again; they will resume their normal dimensions instead of being blown out of proportion.

Use your support systems — your family and friends — to get you through this period. Don't neglect your family in the midst of an obsession with the problem at hand. Even though you should rely on them, do so only in the normal, everyday ways that you always have. Don't use them as a sounding board to vent all your anxieties endlessly.

That was a mistake I made with my family during the Skalbania Enterprises crisis. I'm a talker — I tend to talk things out in order to get them out of my system. Back then I'd go home and say, "Oh God, the bank's going to kill me, they're going to come and take all my money" — and my wife would go crazy with panic. Once I'd talked about it, the problem didn't upset me anymore; it was gone. But she'd stew. To me, losing the family silver or a fancy car or boat is simply not important in the scheme of things. I refuse to become attached to possessions. I operate on the assumption that we'll get others later if we lose the ones we have.

I wouldn't advise everyone who is under stress to come home and tell all to their spouse and kids. It's nice to say that you should share everything, but when you're going through times of stress in your business, sometimes it's better not to. It often means that your support system becomes unstable, because the people in it are upset. Everyone has a different stress-tolerance level, and you have to use your own judgement about choosing the best person to talk to. It might be better to hire a good psychiatrist right from the beginning of the problem; psychiatrists get paid for listening to you. Eugene Kaulius, my CEO, is the man I rely on to vent my anxieties; I can always talk about a problem with him, because he is usually the one dealing with it. It is his responsibility to step in to deal with adversaries at crisis time in my company. His job is to represent me so that I can do my job, which is making money. There should be someone with a job description like Eugene's in your operation.

Don't lose sight of your personal annual goals and resolutions; adhere to them as faithfully as ever.

Take immediate affirmative action when things come into your life that depress you. Remember that how you cope with events in life is more important than the events themselves. It is important that you make positive efforts to regain your financial credibility.

In the early eighties I sold my seventy-two-foot boat for a third of what it was worth. In the same month

I sold my airplane for approximately 75 percent of its value and my car collection and motorcycle at bargain-basement prices. While that was painful at the time, it served to satisfy my bankers that I was serious about cutting costs and paying off my debts. It helped the campaign to forestall bankruptcy. And it was very cleansing for me, too, because now I was no longer responsible for the trimmings that went with those things — the pilot, the taxes, transportation costs, the insurance, the maintenance. I didn't have any fancy toys that creditors could point at to imply that I was bilking them. In the end, I felt fabulous. And I knew that I still had the ability to get my toys back again in the future — in fact, I was sure I would. This period was only a temporary phase, a test of my mettle.

And that attitude didn't apply to my toybox alone. I've been in business for myself for twenty-three years and I have had a net worth of zero at three times in my adult life: age thirty, age thirty-five and age forty-three. In between those times I was a millionaire, as I am today. It is important to keep your reputation and your credibility intact in the down times, so that you can be alive and in business to reap the benefits of the good years. Back off the business scene drastically when times are tough; keep a low profile but stay in business. In 1989 I made $29 million, but only because I stayed whole during the bad years. Don't get exasperated and throw in the towel — retrench.

Quit drinking (and if you do it, smoking) immediately — and for good. Making a decision like that is extremely important, not just because it saves you from alcoholism — or, let's be frank, drug addiction — but because it gives you the conviction that you are in control of a situation that seems to be slipping out of control; you know you are not falling apart if you can make a decision like that. Once you do, it starts to appear a lot more likely that seemingly insurmountable problems are going to be overcome. Whatever your drug of choice — alcohol, pharmaceuticals, cocaine — they are only going to make the problem worse. I knew I could become an alcoholic before the Skalbania crisis was over, so I quit drinking for the entire period I was under stress.

Watch for destructive patterns of behaviour that arise when you're in crisis, whatever they are. Go out and have a good run or work out, instead of going to the bar. You think better when you're exercising — when you're out there running you can think very clearly. I find that if I focus on a problem while I'm running, it seems to resolve itself. Even if there's no solution, it's no help to eat or drink.

During the 1982 crisis I ran the New York marathon and wrote my first book, *Windows of Opportunity*. I deliberately set those two goals to get me back on track, to counter the stress and negativity of fending off bankruptcy.

When you are struck by a serious legal or financial problem, always hire a professional to represent you to your antagonists. Never try to look after it yourself. Then abandon it — dump the problem on your lawyer and focus all your energy on a new venture. Times of turmoil are excellent times to set new personal objectives. Divert your mind from the problem onto a new project where you are working in a positive mode. I started a new business — Triexcellence car dealer-ships — following the Skalbania bankruptcy. It doesn't matter whether the project flies — and this one eventu-ally did not. What matters is that you are not stewing about your crisis or interfering with your lawyer's efforts.

When you are facing tough times it is much better to be working on something, keeping mind and body busy. It's like breaking rocks in jail: wardens don't make prisoners do it because the world needs more rocks; they do it to keep them busy and diffuse stress in a difficult situation. I experienced similar tactics during my years in the army — we dug holes and then we filled them in again. Whenever you have a problem, there is only so much corrective action you can take in any given day. The rest of the day shouldn't be stew time, because that is totally disruptive and degenerative.

Take some advice from Duke Rudman — go to Mexico for a quick change of pace when things get stressful. When negotiations with my creditors were at their hot-test, I took time to go to the beach and rest, concentrat-ing on the cultivation of a positive attitude. It was a good negotiating strategy, a good exercise in mental health and a tremendous relief to my lawyer and my staff.

When you are dealing with problems, the solutions tend to move along at their own speed — they have a momentum you cannot change. Once you have done everything that you can to affect positively a negative situation, you have to be patient and wait for events to unfold. That's the time you should choose to nip away and have a holiday.

Remember that problems are solved one at a time. Have patience. Our nature is to try to solve everything at once, but that will only bring frustration. Ask yourself if this problem will matter ten years from now. Don't lose sight of the big picture. Whenever I feel sorry for myself, I think of the words of Randy Waters, a little boy who lost his arm in a meat grinder: "I don't worry about what I've lost; I concentrate on what I have left."

When we went through the 1981-82 crisis, I wound up with eighteen problematic loans, of which three were in excess of $1 million. I categorized the problem in each case and put the eighteen different projects down on my list every day to look at. Each day I did as much as I could on each one of them and then went on to the next one. This way I could monitor my problems without dwelling on them. It could be done in half an hour and then the rest of the day could be positive.

No matter what the size of your toybox (or what's left of it), dig into it often when you have a problem. My toys are my self-indulgent form of relief from stress — my yacht, my Ferrari collection, my motorcycle, my jet, my helicopter lessons and sky-diving lessons, my car races and mountain bikes. I look at the world and ask, "What are the finest things in this world for man to enjoy? I want to try them all before I die." Indulging in them if you can during times of stress is a real kick.

How well you handle the crises that come your way depends ultimately on how well you have ordered your life beforehand. If you have neglected your family and friends, your physical health or your recreational outlets, you may be heading for trouble. It's really a matter of establishing your values and sticking to them — not only because it is the morally correct thing to do but because it's good for your business and good for you.

Consider your career as a means to an end, not an end in itself. Your professional achievements offer you a measure of self-esteem and pride; they are a source of prestige and worth. Pride and self-worth come from many other aspects of life as well: there are many kinds of achievements, from being a good parent to travelling the world and trying exotic new experiences to volunteering your time for community projects or politics.

The key is to set limits on your professional goals and on the price you are willing to pay to achieve them in terms of their effect on the rest of your life. Cherish the things you treasure before they have slipped away from you or too much damage has been done and it is too late. If I had done things differently in my personal life, I would have spent more time with my children when they were young. If you are not prepared to invest in a relationship, don't have it in your life at all.

When you go through times of stress, the problem causing the stress takes on a larger-than-life prominence. It becomes more important than anything else. I recited the following paragraph to myself a thousand times when I was deep in a financial crisis:

There are many components that comprise life — your family, your work, your friends, your religion, your health, your community interests and your money — all those things and more make up your life. Money is only one of the components of life. Would you rather lose all your money or lose your health? Would you rather lose your family or your money? Money is the easiest thing to lose because you can always get it back.

The reality is that money is the least important thing. Unfortunately, many times when we go into financial crisis, we focus on money as the most important thing in our life.

Treasure and protect your health. Schedule time for physical fitness and watch your diet carefully. You will need a physical release from stress more than ever when you are in crisis. In my case I ran even harder during the collapse of Skalbania Enterprises. Your problems will induce insomnia, but exhausting physical exercise will ensure that you sleep.

In 1988 I injured my back and had to stop running. I have now replaced running with daily bicycle riding. I have a mountain bike and have discovered a whole new world and new friends. Because running was such an enjoyable priority in my life I found it very difficult to admit that my body was no longer equipped to endure the daily punishment. As soon as I found a suitable replacement, it was no longer an issue.

When one door in life closes, you must see it as another door opening. I am now energized and excited about taking a bicycle trip through France. You must accept as you get older the fact that your body won't and can't do what it could in your twenties or thirties. As long as you recognize aging as a fact of life and work with it, you will find it a wonderful adventure, giving you the time to explore worlds and activities you might never have had time for before. That realization was the most important one of my life because maintaining the gift of good health is crucial, especially as we get older. If I were given the choice of getting back my lost

$30 million or regaining my ability to run, there is no doubt which one I would choose. It's all a matter of priorities.

Once I had worked out the terms of my debt payment, I started doing deals immediately to meet those payments and regain my lost ground. I made sure this time that I didn't agree to any terms I couldn't live up to.

I concentrated on doable projects — not the things I wished I could do or wanted to do. I operated more conservatively. I determined that I would push for increased franchise sales and stayed clear of flamboyant megadeals for the time being, concentrating on increasing Century 21's franchise base. I was so single-minded about that that it cost me some profit temporarily. But when the economy recovered and the real estate market improved, our franchise network was in a position to take advantage of it. We did extremely well.

I also made it a rule to complete deals using as little cash as possible from my Century 21 income. Ownership of Century 21 promoted a perception of wealth that enabled me to commit to a purchase with little cash, and then scramble to sell it. Many times I was successful in selling projects either on closing the purchase or shortly thereafter.

In 1988 the remnants of Skalbania Enterprises Limited — really a stack of nearly worthless shares — became Selco Limited, a holding company into which I place many new ventures. This way, I can also take advantage of the tax write-offs that accumulated as a result of earlier losses. To this day no business of mine has ever gone into receivership.

Nevertheless, those losses were an expensive

education. They taught me that I'm an entrepreneurial salesman — that's what I do best, and it's what I should stick to. For a while I lost sight of that. My delusions of grandeur earned me a place in Canadian business history summarized pointedly by Wayne Lilley in *Canadian Business* in 1984:

> He had finally become a peer of the risk takers he'd admired for their willingness to put everything on the table for a single roll. And it almost broke him. . . . Nowhere on the laudatory dust jacket [of his book *Windows of Opportunity*], or in the book for that matter, does Thomas recall how overriding ambition almost bankrupted him.

Now he does.

FOUR

Walking Away: The True Story Behind Heritage USA

FLAWLESS DRIVER, 102
HANGS UP CAR KEYS
"I'd rather quit while I'm ahead," said
William Pettes as he ended his 60-year
driving career without a fender-bender or
even a parking ticket.
— Canadian Press, Knowlton, Quebec

On July 31, 1988, the Charlotte, North Carolina, *Observer* announced that Red Benton, the bankruptcy trustee for the headquarters of Jim and Tammy Bakker's PTL Ministry, Heritage USA, had decided that I had "the financial capability and integrity to take over the assets, and that PTL would like to begin that process" with me next week. On August 7 the Sunday *New York Times* ran a four-column headline: Canadians Make Offer on PTL Ministry and Park. The next day the *Wall Street Journal* picked up the story, and the major U.S. networks were calling. My name was in the international press constantly for months after that. Feature stories in *Maclean's* and the *Financial Times of Canada* followed.

The bankruptcy of Heritage USA had been big

107

news in the international media, and when I read in the paper that the assets were being put up for sale, it looked as if it might be the next deal of the century: a chance to break into the U.S. real estate market in a big way. The project was an extension of the smaller-scale deals I had been doing with Nelson Skalbania. It seemed the logical next step in diversification of my real estate portfolio.

But by November 1988 the deal had gone sour, and in December the property was awarded to Torontonian Stephen Mernick. In April 1989 the Toronto *Globe and Mail*'s "Street Talk" columnist Bud Jorgensen summarized the situation succinctly:

> On the buy side is an orthodox Jew; the development itself is in bankruptcy as a result of infighting (and infidelity) among fundamentalist Christians; and the park is located on land to which North American Indians are trying to register a prior claim. . . .

> The latest twist in the plot is an announcement earlier this week that the park is about to lose a major tenant, Heritage Ministries. . . . The park itself is "languishing." The hotel is only at 10 percent occupancy and repairs are badly needed. . . . Efforts to contact [the winning bidder, Torontonian Stephen] Mernick or his lawyers result in referrals to one of two PR consultants — Tom Reid in Toronto or Alex Coffin in Charlotte. . . . Neither Mr. Reid nor Mr. Coffin has any information on when the sale might close.

It never did. Stephen Mernick pulled out on September 20, 1989 — one day before he was to reveal his financial records to the PTL bankruptcy court. Eventually he announced that he was broke and living off his mother-in-law. At the end of 1990 the *Financial Times of Canada* ran a feature on him headed: "The would-be developer prince has been grounded by a host of ugly allegations and a legion of lawsuits." Some of his assets were in receivership or bankruptcy, and his debts were said to be at least $80 million.

Unbeknownst to others, like William Pettes I had hung up my car keys and quit while I was ahead a long time before. In the intervening months Heritage USA had forsaken the road to salvation in favour of the path to limbo, and I had had a great ride.

First, the public story. At the time Heritage USA went bankrupt in 1987, the PTL Ministry owed at least $110 million and possibly as much as $275 million U.S. to creditors and the federal government.

After some preliminary negotiations, on July 22, 1988, Samoth Capital offered $113 million U.S. for Heritage USA. On August 5 the offer was accepted. Bankruptcy trustee Red Benton and I signed a tentative letter of agreement, which included a cash payment of $46 million, a promissory note for $49 million, and an $18 million debenture with a seven-year no-interest payback. September 1 was set as the deadline for competing offers.

On August 31 Red Benton announced that Jim Bakker had made an offer of $172 million U.S. Not only was it higher than mine, the PTL flock would not allow Benton to ignore a chance to resurrect their leader. Benton gave Bakker until September 9 to come up with a $3 million deposit and proof that he could get the rest.

On September 2, the day after the bidding deadline, Benton did something that amounted to the straw that broke the camel's back: he took out an ad in the *Wall Street Journal* seeking additional bids. I announced that I was tired of having my offer used as the target for other people to shoot at, especially when bids as flaky as Jimmy Bakker's were being taken seriously. I withdrew my offer.

While other bids were coming in, it was discovered that Bakker's was being backed by Louis Pihakis, who had a long criminal record. Bakker never did come up with his deposit.

On September 9, I resubmitted my offer for $113 million. At least two other bidders were in the running. Thirty-four-year-old Toronto real estate developer Stephen Mernick was one of them, with an offer of $115 million.

On September 27 Red Benton postponed the bankruptcy court hearing at which his reacceptance of my offer was to be ruled upon.

On October 4 it was announced to the media that Stephen Mernick's offer was accepted. He agreed to come up with $50 million in cash and pay the rest over five years. He had thirty days to do his due diligence; in other words, to review the account books and inspect the grounds to ensure that the property measured up to its owners' representations of it.

Mernick's offer, which still had to go to bankruptcy court for approval, made many of the major creditors nervous; they didn't think he could come up with the promised funds. On October 25 a number of them jointly filed a motion with the court in South Carolina, calling on it to consider approval of Samoth's offer as an alternative to his. The motion was scheduled to be heard on November 16, when the court would also consider the trustee's recommendation in favour of the Mernick offer. Among the creditors who filed the motion were the Official Unsecured Creditors Committee, the Official PTL Lifetime Partners Committee, the Rock Hill National Bank and the National City Bank of Minneapolis. The two financial institutions, major backers of Heritage USA, were among the secured creditors who had to be paid before the Christian faithful ever saw a dime — which was highly unlikely.

In late October Samoth issued a press release that chortled on about how happy we were to reinstate our old offer.

On November 17 the Columbia, South Carolina, *State* trumpeted the banner headline: PTL Sell-off Ordered:

> A court hearing on the sale of the foundering television ministry ended in pandemonium when Judge Rufus W. Reynolds set his own conditions.

> The main one is that the prospective buyer cannot walk away before closing with little financial loss. The purchaser must assume full liability 30 days after the order approving the sale, the judge said.

Rufus Reynolds, the oldest bankruptcy judge in the United States of America, was sitting on his last case and was fiercely determined to bring it to a speedy and successful conclusion. He was absolutely untouchable, no matter what he decided — no one was going to take on Rufus. The judge had rejected not only Samoth's reinstated offer, but Mernick's, too; both of us seemed to have seen the error of our ways and included escape hatches in the form of final-subject clauses in our final offers and he wouldn't accept that. Judge Reynolds, who treated everyone present with the courtly demeanor a master displays toward his servants, scheduled an auction for the following morning in the hall outside the courtroom in Columbia. The Toronto *Globe and Mail* covered the November 18 auction and reported:

> Lawyer Ed Allman declared the auction open at 9:30 and was greeted by complete silence. About five minutes later, acknowledging that the bid failed to meet the judge's conditions, Mr. Thomas's spokesman put an all-cash $70 million deal on the table.
>
> Mr. Allman rejected it but said it was useful "for information." After several more minutes, Joseph Kluttz, acting for Mr. Mernick, asked for an hour's delay because his client's father-in-law had died late Wednesday and he had not had time to give sufficient thought to restrictions imposed by the judge. When the session resumed after the recess, Mr. Kluttz offered only minor modifications to his proposal.
>
> It was a standoff, and Judge Reynolds was philosophical from the bench. "I was trying to get them while they had the fever," he said with a shrug, setting December 13 as the date finally to decide the case.

The final chapter in the saga includes these facts that are common knowledge: Stephen Mernick never closed the deal and, until December 1990, neither did anyone else; Jimmy Bakker is in jail. The grounds have long been off-limits to all but residents. Evidently there has been vandalism, and the site has fallen into decay. Early in 1991 it was still under heavy guard and over-grown with weeds.

The story that few people know about follows. I like to call it the Red and Rufus Show, after Red Benton — the frail, elderly Southern gentleman who served as bankruptcy trustee — and Rufus Reynolds, the thoroughly exasperated judge who had presided over this little circus for the better part of a year.

As the Red and Rufus Show progressed in true Southern style, all kinds of gremlins came out of the woodwork, as often happens in such high-profile deals. All of a sudden people are not who they once said they were, and other people say there are deals with you that you have never heard of. In the beginning I had American legal counsel who later insisted that I sign a form saying that they never were my counsel, to protect themselves from their own conflict of interest; and a certain Californian insisted that I promised a $1.5 million "finder's fee" and a TV show for putting me on to the PTL deal — as if everybody on planet Earth had not been aware of it! Almost everyone, it seemed, claimed to have an "in" with the trustee or the ministry or the government that would clinch the deal for me.

After my offer for the property was accepted in August 1988, I asked my former boss at the Principal Group, Ken Marlin, to go down and take a look at it; he was just recovering from the crash of the Cormie empire. This deal required hard work to assess whether it was a good one or not. We had to ferret out the facts, because they were not obvious and we could not believe what we were told. No one associated with the property really knew exactly what it was worth. The creditors were demanding nothing less than $113 million, the amount required to cover all debts.

On my initial trip down there I had looked up the only other serious contender, Southern entrepreneur George Shinn, who owned, among other things, a local basketball team. He was a Good Ol' Boy, and I was sure that if he wanted the property he could have it for the asking. I had to make sure that I wasn't being used to drive up the bidding. When I met with Shinn he indicated that all he really required was some of the undeveloped land on which to build a sports stadium; if he couldn't get the property at a fire-sale price, he really wasn't interested. We agreed that there would be no point to bidding against each other and that he could buy the land for his stadium from me at a good price, should I be the winning bidder. Shortly thereafter, he dropped out of the running.

I asked Ken to do my due diligence for me. He was to be my trusted second on that deal, the person whom I consulted before removing the final-subject clauses on my August offer. He was not only elated with what he found there, but also overjoyed that he had found a second career after the disaster he had just left behind. Word came back from him after a week that it was all systems go — Heritage USA could be the deal of a lifetime, but he stressed we had to undertake a more detailed evaluation of several factors affecting the terms of purchase.

As a result of Ken's assessment Eugene Kaulius headed down to take a closer look. It wasn't too long before he was concerned with the viability of the project at the $113 million price. The two of them spent a total of three weeks down there in October and November of

1988, and Eugene assisted Ken in evaluating the proposition from several points of view. It became clear by the end of that time that we had not fully considered all the ramifications of the purchase. Their joint recommendation was that we not proceed with it — at least not on the terms originally proposed. The value of the project lay in its undeveloped land rather than in the existing development. The place was not worth anywhere near $113 million; their best estimate was a maximum of $70 million, so we made an offer on November 18 for that amount.

They came to that conclusion because the existing development, which they noted is located "in the middle of nowhere" twelve miles out of Charlotte, North Carolina, had six million people visit it in 1986 who had done so exclusively because it was a religious retreat. Everything that took place there was tied to the religious theme, and the traffic to Heritage USA was created solely by the charisma of its founders, Jimmy and Tammy. But the operation on its own was not profitable — it was not set up to make money. It was all done purely for show, to attract donations to the ministry. Profit was realized only from the television fund-raising appeals of Jimmy Bakker, not from the attractions, shops and real estate.

The ministry had brought something like $400 million to that site through fund-raising, and they'd put over $200 million into developing it. It was exciting on the face of it: there were over 2,000 acres, 1,000 homes, condominiums, time-sharing units, a shopping mall, the best TV production facilities in America, a telephone exchange system said to be equal to the Pentagon's, an entertainment park, sports facilities, a water park and two big hotels — it was awesome. Impressive as the development was, what attracted me was the fact that 90 percent of the acreage was yet to be developed.

But without the religious base, who would want to come to a development in that location? Without a charismatic leader like Jimmy Bakker, how successful would a Christian theme park be? The fund-raising that financed the operation was already in disarray — especially since his actions had alienated many followers from the ministry. What's more, there was a secular theme park, Carowinds, nearby, so there was little market for another one.

When we took a closer look, we started asking how much the hotels cost, how much the development was worth and how much the undeveloped land was worth. How much were the homes selling for? Why were those people there? Why were they in a settlement in this location? There was no dramatic landscape or waterfront — the site had no resort atmosphere. If people came strictly for the religious theme, was there any reason to be there otherwise? Take the religious theme away — and unless we kept it, we wouldn't have all those people — and the value wasn't there. If we kept the religious theme we would have to dance to Heritage Ministries' tune; and then we wouldn't be able to make it work financially.

We assessed the price-per-acre the property was worth in the marketplace, without the religious element, based on what we thought people would be prepared to pay to rent or buy there, or to stay in the hotels. If we could get it at a price that would be profitable, could we service the debt?

We decided that if we sold the property tomorrow without the religious base, its cash value would be something like $70 million. The most we'd consider offering in a revised bid was $50 million, because I had to have a cushion of $20 million above what I paid for it. Unless we had $20 million for maintenance and development funds, we shouldn't do the deal. That made the ideal, realistic price $50 million, even though we had offered $70 million.

The $20 million was for the unknowns; there were so many variables. If we didn't cater to the religious following, then we had no ready market — we had to start from ground zero. But my biggest single concern was the extent of the deterioration of the site, caused by a year of non-maintenance. The property was falling apart at a rapid rate, the residents were moving away and the number of visitors had dropped drastically. If a deal wasn't closed quickly, even that $70 million value would have to be reassessed.

I was in an extremely difficult position. Four months earlier, on August 16, I had stood at Heritage USA in what was once the most celebrated studio of TV evangelism. A crowd of five hundred people gave me a cheering, standing ovation. In the immense hall where Jimmy Bakker had once held sway, I made a speech to the assembled PTL devotees promising to attempt to continue the religious theme of the park. I told them:

> I have found that it would conflict with my own conscience to pursue a course that would destroy the unique and remarkable environment that has been created here at Heritage USA. Yet, for me to simply walk away from Heritage USA I have found equally unacceptable. I do not feel I can turn my back without making an effort to preserve the concepts created here.

> I am both pleased and proud to announce that I

have met with the executives of Heritage Ministries and with the trustee, Mr. M.C. Benton, and
have committed to them on behalf of Samoth Capital Corporation, my publicly owned merchant
banking enterprise, the following:

1. Samoth Capital Corporation *will* maintain Heritage USA as a Christian theme park and conference centre that encompasses traditional family
   values.

2. I will work with the Heritage Ministries to allow
   them continued use of the twenty-four-hour
   Inspirational Network. I will give facilities to a
   new Heritage church on this site and will maintain certain other religious facilities.

3. I vow that no alcohol or tobacco products will
   ever be sold on the Heritage USA grounds.

We will meet as quickly as possible to determine
whether or not a feasible, businesslike plan to pre-
serve Heritage USA as a Christian retreat centre
and sanctuary can be accomplished before the
assets deteriorate any further or the trustee
decides to liquidate.

That last paragraph was intended as a signal to the
devotees that nothing was certain except uncertainty.
Although we were committed to banning alcohol and
tobacco, Red Benton and I already suspected that an
exclusively Christian park might not survive; we envi-
sioned preserving Heritage Ministries on a small part of
the property and developing a Canyon Ranch-style
health centre and secular residential complex on the
rest. We signed a confidential document to that effect
the very next day. It read in part:

Samoth and its principals have, since August 9,
1988, been on the PTL premises to conduct their
due diligence review and investigation of PTL.
Although their review and investigations on
behalf of Samoth have only begun, it has become
apparent that PTL cannot and should not be purchased and operated as a non-secular enterprise.

What followed was a proposal, presented to Judge
Rufus Reynolds, to organize the site under the aegis of a
"new publicly held for-profit corporation."

In my speech I was trying to let the thousands of
people who had an emotional and financial stake in the
place know that we meant well and had their best interests at heart. We were trying to bring them around
slowly to the fact that we had to come up with a feasible
compromise that would find a home for them on the
site while converting it to a sound, for-profit business
venture. I was determined not to let these people down.
What we hoped to do was turn over a portion of the
property, including the church and dormitories, to Heritage Ministries as a home base for PTL members. We
would also give them access to the television facilities at
special discount rates.

"God can stay as long as He pays the rent," I told
them.

On August 22 I circulated a memo to key Samoth
board members spelling out how we would begin to
pull off the resurrection of Heritage USA once we took
possession. It read in part:

PRIORITIES

1. Immediately assess the assets and stop the bleed-
   ing. PHT will be team leader. We need a hotel

person, a land development person and a TV person.

2. We must develop financing strategy — a partner with deep pockets, a syndicate, a loan and a public stock issue. Try to do a New York stock exchange public issue before closing. We need $46 million U.S. to close and a commitment to $20 million U.S. to finish the highrise hotel and clean up the deferred maintenance. We also need funds to hire a new team. At present there are 16,000 man hours donated per month.

We had the perfect talent pool to pull it off in our key Samoth board members. Jack Gilbert is a seasoned business lawyer who has been my trusted friend and confidante since my involvement with Samoth Capital Corporation. Karsten von Wersebe, the aloof and reserved head of the York-Hannover Group of real estate companies — including principal operating companies in Toronto, New York, Lucerne and Munich — is the equal of anyone in the world when it comes to real estate development and has special expertise in entertainment parks. His support was the key factor in this deal, and he thought the property was a bargain that had the potential to produce $1 billion a year for Samoth if properly developed. Stuart Henry is a finance and stock-market specialist currently with First Marathon Securities Limited. Together we were ready to pull it off.

I had originally offered $113 million; within the month we had backed off. In the meantime Jimmy Bakker had made his offer, we had withdrawn ours, he had been sent packing and we had reinstated ours.

On September 19 we met with trustee Red Benton. We were assured that Red was prepared to work exclusively with us to develop an agreement that we would jointly submit to the court. We presented him with our proposal for salvaging the site, called the Heritage Corporation Concept Paper. It stated at the outset that we believed that the Christian theme of the park was "essential to the future success of Heritage USA":

> In the United States alone, the Christian movement is represented by more than 70 million people. . . . Moreover, many of the values and ideals that are inherent in the Christian lifestyle are beginning to be adopted more and more as part of the mainstream American lifestyle. Current demographic trends point toward an aging population. Older people tend to seek more security, safety and tranquility. The baby-boom generation is developing new lifestyle attitudes that are more conservative and health-conscious. Advances in technology and structural changes in the economy are leading people to seek new outlets for their increasing leisure time. These are trends that could be of value in planning a development and marketing strategy for Heritage USA.

The paper further provided for development in three specific areas — the undeveloped real estate, the theme park and the satellite cable network.

REAL ESTATE
The Heritage USA development includes more than 1,800 acres of prime developable land within the natural path of the development of Charlotte, North Carolina. We would propose that the plan for the real estate focus on new residential development. Quality single-family housing could be

NEVER FIGHT WITH A PIG

set amongst a country-club-style development, combined with condominium retirement villas appealing to the emerging upper-middle-income seniors' market.

FAMILY PARK
We would propose that we undertake further improvement of the family park's assets and develop the park as a major fitness, health and recreation centre. Quality accommodation would be available in all price ranges. The centrepiece of the development would be the high-tech health and fitness facilities and the related services available. A major lifestyles clinic would be situated in these facilities, staffed by professionals in a number of disciplines, including medical professionals, qualified fitness and nutrition specialists, and lifestyle consultants.

SATELLITE CABLE NETWORK
The existing network and related facilities provide access to more than 10 million U.S. homes via the Galaxy 1 satellite. We would propose that the modern production facilities be utilized both for contract work and for in-house production of programming. The programming produced would be lifestyles-oriented and aimed at the target market described earlier. The themes of the programming would be consistent with those used to market the other facilities and we would strive to maximize the educational and informational content.

Under the timely disclosure policy of the Toronto Stock Exchange, we were not allowed to reveal these plans to the press, who by this time were hounding us without interruption. It was imperative that everyone have equal access to information, and that we notify the wire services and the marketplace after the signing of the deal and the closing of the market on the day of signing. Only then could we issue a press release or call a press conference. From that day forward, everything took place behind locked doors.

We engaged a law firm to prepare a draft agreement and I had extensive discussions with Red Benton and his counsel that resulted in a draft definitive agreement to purchase the PTL assets. It specified conditions that would either allow me to revise the deal down the road if the value proved inflated, or would get the deal thrown out of court. We wanted the opportunity to be able to revise the purchase price downward and come at the deal more realistically without jeopardizing our chances of winning.

We expected Red Benton to sign this September 26 agreement and submit it to the court on September 27. When he failed to live up to this commitment, we suspected negotiations were taking place with another bidder.

As late as Friday, September 30, we believed that we had an opportunity to reach an agreement with Benton. On Monday, October 3, late in the day, we were informed that he planned to announce the next day that he had reached an agreement with Mr. Mernick.

By the time the two offers were thrown out of court in November, Eugene Kaulius and Ken Marlin had determined that the purchase was really not a real estate deal as we had hoped but a business-operation deal that was fraught with problems, and it would require a considerable commitment of time and resources. Something had to be done with the undeveloped property, and existing roads, water, utilities and attendant property taxes had to be paid for by very few revenue producers. Ken and Eugene summarized their findings to me in a confidential memo.

The most significant revenue producer was the TV satellite, but in the trustee period it had lost 2.2 million subscribers. Moreover, cable distribution was on a month-to-month basis and vulnerable to quick movement by the cable distributors from one channel to another. Although there was a great deal of potential to produce substantial revenue in the state-of-the-art studio with its excellent technical expertise, there were few programming directors as well as an alarming lack of ongoing marketing. The number of TV subscribers was shrinking, the programming was often reduced to repeats and fund-raisers, the new minister was not charismatic and there was a danger of losing channel position with some of the cable systems, whose bills were not being paid.

The Heritage Grand Hotel could also be a revenue producer, but it would operate with one hand tied behind its back if we tried to do it as we intended within Christian parameters — with no drinking or smoking and observation of Christian worship services. The magnificent water park could produce income only on a seasonal basis.

Because the resort was so far from the Charlotte area, the need for extensive residential development was several years away. At the time of sale, the park did not have sufficient theme attractions to be a viable business. As a result it would of necessity continue to depend totally on the fundamentalist Christians for financial support. But Jimmy Bakker's scandals had driven away so many of them that a recent telethon had not raised enough money to pay for the TV rental time.

The only clientele in the immediate future would be the Christian one, but it would be impossible to run the operation on a for-profit basis and keep them happy. We slowly began to realize that there would most likely be regular interference by them in the daily operations. For example, it was suggested to us at one point that the water-park recreation area have a dress code, and that the pool be closed during church services. Moreover, the Christians were not big spenders in the shops.

Vacancies were on the increase in the condos; any effort to increase sales and rentals would have to appeal to non-Christians, which would probably inspire the wrath of the residents. Staffing would be costly and fraught with tension if and when a commercially oriented group gradually took over from the holdovers from Jimmy Bakker's time.

Taking all these factors into consideration, Eugene advised that if we succeeded in purchasing the property for $50 million, potential losses at the outset would be approximately $1 million per month. An equity issue or immediate property sale would be essential; since putting any of the property up for sale in the immediate future would require selling at distress prices, the only choices we would have left were to raise equity or sell the television station.

As an anonymous lawyer in the bankruptcy proceedings told the Charlotte *Observer* on December 11, "We've taken this dog and put it up in the show, and it ain't won anything."

In the same article local real estate developers said that not only was the development "too far out in the country, but what is already at Heritage USA makes it less attractive." One of them noted, "I don't think it's an income-producing business. The income came from Jim Bakker's ability to talk people into sending him money, not for any value received, necessarily." The conclusion, run in a twenty-point headline, was: PTL Is Not a Hot Property.

Eugene Kaulius arrived in Charlotte the day before that article appeared. He had been invited down there by Heritage Ministries, which represented the Christian flock, to attempt to work out a partnership agreement with them to make a joint offer for the assets. His mission was to determine how Samoth could act as finance obtainers, property managers and developers for them in their role as an independent, religious arm of PTL created after the bankruptcy to try to save Heritage USA.

They were led by the Reverend Samuel Johnson, pastor of Heritage Village Church and known as Pastor Sam. The inheritor of Jimmy Bakker's tattered mantle, Sam was the consummate Christian clergyman, a mustachioed, handsome young man who made every effort to be of service and to look after the spiritual interests of his followers. When it came to the fiscal end of the burden he was saddled with, he was stretched pretty thin. He had a board of solid businessmen, but they were part-timers who seemed to show up only long enough to change his mind, over and over again.

Now the Red and Rufus Show also had Pastor Sam, and what a jolly triumvirate they were.

Eugene met with Pastor Sam on Saturday and on Sunday morning, in preparation for the bidding session at Red's office on Monday, December 12 and Rufus's court hearing on December 13. It was agreed that

Eugene would attend both. The strategy was that Heritage Ministries would qualify themselves as a bidder by providing a $1 million refundable deposit, with sixty days to close. They would top the highest bid by $1 million, subject to on-the-spot discussions with Pastor Sam and Eugene. Pastor Sam went away to discuss this strategy with the board and promised to get back to Eugene later that day.

Eugene went back to his hotel room and waited for a phone call. And waited. And waited. He tried all day to get through to Pastor Sam, but could not. He did not even go out to eat in case that call came. It was nine o'clock at night before the phone rang: he was asked to meet with the board immediately. He had no idea what he was walking into; all he knew was that the board and Sam had already positioned themselves.

According to Eugene, the meeting was the most pressurized, emotionally-fraught business event he had ever attended in his life. The board had just spent two weeks undertaking a fund-raising campaign to come up with $5 million to put down on the deal. Over and over again, until two in the morning each night, they had to take turns keeping viewers high and keeping that money coming in. When the goal wasn't reached, they had to go back again and again and ask people to dig a little deeper. Viewers were sending in their silverware and jewellery. When the board finally reached their goal, a tremendous, hysterical cheer went up.

Now Pastor Sam had to lead this group of men in deciding how to dispose of the money and who to go into partnership with. By the time Eugene walked into that meeting room, every one of those men was stretched to the breaking point. Everything they had struggled for for so long would come to a head the next morning in Red Benton's office.

They had decided to change the terms of the deal altogether; they would not present themselves as partners with Samoth, and there was no time to discuss it further. They claimed they had to keep their options open. What they didn't understand was that partners have to go into a courtroom bidding situation with a firm, detailed strategy and a clear mutual understanding of precisely where they stand. In court, all sorts of unexpected things could and would happen, and they had to be ready for them. But there was no time left to convince them of this, and no room for a joint strategy because there were no partners.

Early on Monday morning Pastor Sam, members of the board and Eugene met to review a press release stating that Heritage Ministries was "in the process of completing an agreement with the Samoth Capital Corporation, Vancouver, Canada, that would allow Heritage Ministries, Inc. to complete the purchase of Heritage USA." If all went well and Samoth won, it was to be distributed immediately after the bidding was ended.

Then Sam and Eugene drove to the trustee's office to attend the auction. Along the way, Eugene was able to chat with Sam and discuss some of the strategy that they had not been able to deal with the night before. But as soon as they arrived, the board members took poor Sam aside and told him that there were no guarantees — there was no commitment to working in tandem. Although they were predisposed to Samoth, they couldn't guarantee not to throw in their $5 million with a higher bidder.

The trustee started the bidding at $80 million.

There were no offers.

He dropped it quickly to $70 million. The tension in the room was horrific.

Still there were no offers, and bidding was adjourned.

There was shock and palpable emotional upheaval all around. No one had expected that things would get so bad. The judge had made it clear that he would accept nothing lower than $50 to $60 million.

During the adjournment Eugene called me in Vancouver to discuss strategy, and we decided that we wouldn't be used simply to drive up the bidding. We stood our ground. We were there, as far as we were concerned, to support Heritage Ministries in their decision, whatever that was.

After the adjournment Behakel Corporation, local TV station owners — representing the interests of George Shinn, the local entrepreneur who had backed out of the bidding at the outset — opened up the bidding at around $20 million and were immediately increased by Stephen Mernick. The process continued until bidding stopped at $35.25 million — Mernick's offer. There was another adjournment.

Eugene considered entering the bidding on behalf of Samoth, but decided to stick with the existing strategy. When trustee Red Benton resumed his chair, he stated emphatically that Judge Rufus Reynolds would never accept the Mernick bid. Several bidders, including Eugene, were invited to meet with the creditors in an effort to elicit bids.

All that evening Eugene met with the full board of the ministry as well as Pastor Sam. It was clear to him that they wanted to make a deal with us rather than with Mernick. Even though Mernick had interceded during the evening to offer them guaranteed use of the church facilities and the television station, the board stayed to negotiate with Eugene rather than leaving to see Mernick. The following deal was worked out:

1. Samoth would bid up to $53 million.

2. The ministry would put up a non-refundable $1 million deposit, which Samoth would guarantee.

3. The purchase would be on a joint basis whereby Samoth would be entitled to 75 percent interest in the project and the ministry 25 percent. Any price above $50 million would be paid totally by the ministry without any change in their percentage.

4. On closing in sixty days the ministry agreed to buy, at mutually agreed appraised values, the church, the prayer room, the amphitheatre, the fort and the girls' building. All were non-income-producing facilities and their sale would have provided $3-$5 million in cash for working capital.

5. The TV operations would be under joint management for three years, at the end of which time we would give the ministry an option to buy it at fair market value.

6. Samoth would manage all the other properties and hotels as well as act as property developers, and would receive an appropriate management fee for same.

7. Because the financing may have required some equity dilution, it was understood that the dilution would be proportionate to both parties.

Meanwhile, Heritage Ministries released the memo we had reviewed earlier that morning, changing the words "the Samoth Capital Corporation, Vancouver, Canada" to "several investors."

With the agreement in place, Eugene attended the court hearing on Tuesday. Red Benton's lawyers conveyed the unsatisfactory results of the bidding to Judge Reynolds.

Then Red stunned all present with the announcement that he and the board had met with Stephen Mernick and his lawyers the previous evening. Unknown to Eugene, the board must have left their meetings with him to go into another session. Mernick had increased his bid to $65 million with a 5 percent cash deposit, subject to certain conditions.

There was pandemonium among the creditors' lawyers and the Behakel camp. One lawyer jumped up to object strenuously that there was no indication that Mr. Mernick had either a track record in property management or the ability to raise the cash. The judge would have none of it, but said that no matter what, the sale must close by September 1989 or the deal would be cancelled.

Behakel's lawyer suddenly jumped up to offer $70 million, but the judge ruled that since they were not the highest bidder on the previous day, their offer was inadmissible. The lawyers for the unsecured creditors and for Behakel objected again, but the judge simply reminded them that they could appeal his order — which was highly unlikely given the reputation of Rufus.

When Stephen Mernick made his $65 million bid, back in Vancouver Ken Marlin told me immediately that he'd never close, because he wouldn't be able to get anyone to back it. My decision was to sit back and wait for the agreement to fall apart, and see what kind of deal I could strike afterwards.

It was a matter of bowing out gracefully at that point. At an initial court hearing to approve our bid in August we had made a bid that we didn't really want them to take and it was worded accordingly. I had made up my mind about that before the offers went to court for approval. I had decided that unless I could get the place at a rock-bottom figure, I didn't want it. The decision was made before Mernick was awarded the property, in consultation with Eugene and Ken, as well as lawyer Jack Gilbert and developer Karsten von Wersebe, and we all agreed.

The fact is that few judges, unless they have been business people, understand how to elicit bids. They are used to ruling the roost in their courtroom. Judge Reynolds did not seem to understand that he couldn't simply command people to bid more money, according to his schedule. A business person will just walk away and come back if and when he is ready.

But the real fault lay with his adviser, trustee Red Benton, who should have known a good deal when he saw it. He was the one who advised the judge of the best party for the property. As a public official, Red was in an extremely difficult position, because the primary item on his agenda was the perception among all interest groups that he was executing his public trust properly. Before Red Benton made any move he had to look over his shoulder to see what everyone else thought. The perception that justice was being served was critical. It was better for him to let Samoth's offer go than to face the wrath of those who objected to it at any point along the way.

Red was not free to simply use his discretion in selecting the best offer and partnering it, for fear that another, better one might come up. His decision-making abilities were hampered by pressure groups he had to appease at all costs. If the pressure was to go with the highest bidder no matter who or what his credentials, Red Benton didn't have much choice in the matter.

What I got out of the experience was a huge legal bill and a lot of publicity of incalculable value — and all publicity is good publicity. Because of the public exposure, I have a lot of investment projects submitted to me for consideration. When I talked about the deal publicly in advance of clinching it, I risked looking as if I had lost; but the risk has paid off handsomely. What is important is that I did not get so caught up in the euphoria and the ego trip — in the emotional attachment to the deal — that I pursued it at all costs.

I let deals wear themselves out, because most of the time things change rapidly. Had Mernick not bid as he did, then the property would probably have fallen into my lap at the right price. If the trustee and the judge had been smart enough to see that Mernick would never close, or if they had pulled the plug on him sooner, they might have come back to me, and it could have been a wonderful deal. I certainly didn't want to say anything negative about the property or its associates to prevent that from happening.

Every deal is the right deal at the right price. I would have loved to pull that one together and bring it back to life on a new basis and a sound financial footing. I had grandiose dreams for the place that got me excited just thinking about them: an idyllic collection of single-family homes, retirement villas, top-notch hotels and a high-tech health and fitness facility like the Canyon Ranch.

The irony of it all is the fact that in the end the property was sold for $42.5 million U.S. — $7.5 million less than the amount we had offered in 1988. On Friday, December 14, 1990, the new owner, San Diego evangelist Morris Cerullo, closed the deal. He renamed the property New Heritage USA, promising to reopen in summer 1991. Before he can do that, according to his own estimate at least $15 million in restoration will be needed.

An intriguing footnote is the fact that one of Cerullo's three financial backers, he says, is "Seraphim Corporation of Vancouver, British Columbia." All he would reveal about the three investors beyond their corporate names is that they "have extensive involvement in hotel ownership. These are all Christian people, they are all evangelical, born-again, spirit-filled people. They do not want the limelight."

After the deal closed Cerullo's backers were revealed to be four Malaysian businessmen who own 51 percent of the park. In March 1991, they filed a fraud and conspiracy lawsuit against him. The twenty-one-page suit, which had 300 pages of depositions and affidavits attached, accused Cerullo of improperly funnelling $4 million raised from 14,300 contributors into an escrow account that he personally controlled on behalf of his ministry. The suit also claimed that the money was raised through a discount membership program that was initiated before the new backers came on board but that Cerullo only inadvertently informed them of its existence much later. Cerullo vehemently denied the accusations, claiming that the suit contained "factual errors, contradictions and wholly unsupportable legal suppositions." In spite of the dispute, New Heritage President Yet-King Loy insisted at the time of launching the suit that the group was going forward with preparations for an early summer opening.

NEGOTIATING STRATEGIES

The negotiations for Heritage USA were more complicated and fraught with intrigue than most. The normal course of negotiations should run more smoothly. Below are some tips drawn from my experiences.

For any negotiations, remember to document everything. Although it seems obvious, many people simply neglect to put their oral agreements on paper. When you have a meeting to discuss a deal, take notes, and confirm those notes in a follow-up document I usually refer to as a "Memorandum of Understanding," which you should ask the other party to co-sign. Make sure that you are careful to restrict your letter to an expression of intention to proceed in good faith on the basis of the points in the letter, subject to formal agreements to be drawn up by professional advisers and executed later. Always conclude a business meeting by saying that you will confirm the details of the meeting in a letter the following day — just make sure that it is clearly stated that it is not a legally binding letter.

When I closed the Century 21 deal with Art Bartlett on the back of a pad of paper, he was the one at risk, not me. He was the one with the most at stake, and I was just a beginner. Now I am usually the biggest participant in any deal and it is much more important for me to document things than it is for the other guy.

The main reason for documentation is the fact that

North America is extremely litigious compared to a country like Japan, for instance. Japan has only 14,000 lawyers — or about one for every 9,000 people — as opposed to one lawyer for every 320 people in the United States. Japanese transactions are based on honour and trust. In Canada, a buyer could have tied Art Bartlett up in court for years with that deal that we scrawled on a scrap of cardboard. If I had decided to flip it, for instance, or if he had had second thoughts about the sale, we might still be fighting about it.

In addition, it is important to write down the deal exactly as you understand it simply because many times the opposite sides in a negotiation are hearing different things to what is actually being said, and you are both making different assumptions. Often enough, things are simply not discussed. There is no villain and no one is lying.

Once you have done the preliminaries — including all your homework and a comprehensive business plan — then the real negotiation with the other party begins. Now you begin to structure the deal with the vendor or purchaser. A purchaser can negotiate hard on one of two things: either price or terms. In my opinion, the most important aspect of any deal is the terms. I always negotiate harder on those.

The terms that are important to you change according to the phase your career is in. When I first started out in real estate, I made a point of negotiating the lowest possible cash deposit — that was my primary goal and if I didn't get the deposit low enough, I didn't buy. Later I offered a high cash deposit and pushed for a lower selling price. Now I often offer all cash in exchange for the lowest price I can get.

Let the other party state their price first. When you do that, as the unknown factor in the equation you retain control of the direction of the negotiations. Learn to use that fact to your advantage. The first party to name a figure is forever on the defensive, and inevitably has to compromise. Once you are seen to compromise or to be willing to do so, you lose the advantage. The other party also assumes that the figure you have named is higher than what you expect to end up with if you are the seller, or lower if you are the buyer. You have in effect revealed and therefore weakened your position — given away your ace in the hole — whereas the other party has not.

Never make a firm offer that exceeds the market value. If you want an example of what happens when you do that, have a look at the career of retailing magnate Robert Campeau. His ambition blinded him — and, by the way, several major financial institutions — to the dangers of exceeding the current market value. He fell in love with an asset and didn't look hard enough at the down side. As Sam Belzberg, founder of First City Trust, has said many times, if you risk a dollar to make a dollar, that is not a good enough return for the risk you take. Campeau risked many dollars indeed for the prestige of being a major player in the U.S. market, with little thought to cash flow. His fall has been followed most recently by that of Donald Trump, who went down for the same reason: he financed his empire with borrowed money — loans reported by the Associated Press as "believed to total more than $3 billion." Your ability to repay a loan is only as good as the economy, which you cannot control.

Sometimes it can be an effective negotiating strategy to make an offer that exceeds the market value —

with several conditions attached to it. That gets the vendor motivated and establishes rapport and momentum — everyone is enthusiastic. Slowly, as the conditions begin to prove shaky, the offer comes down to something more realistic; but by then you've got them hooked. They have probably set aside other parties to negotiate solely with you and they aren't going to start all over again.

The term of primary importance is the time frame: you want to negotiate for as long a time as possible before you have to put down substantial amounts of money. It is amazing what facts will come out of the woodwork with the benefit of enough time to uncover them. I've done many deals on the basis of a dollar down, with a very long time before I had to close.

If you want to know the true meaning of *tempus fugit* (time flies), sign a thirty-day note. You may think thirty days is a long time to allow before you have to close, but when you sign the deal and leave the room, suddenly all the people you need to talk to — your lawyer, your bank manager, your accountant — are out of town. You have to structure your deal so that you will not be backed into a corner, and go for as much time as you can get. You can convince the vendor that because you are improving his land through such things as rezoning, if you walk away from the deal you will have increased the value of his land. It can take years to get the necessary clearances and approvals to develop a property; if they don't go through, you will want the right to walk away from the deal on the closing date.

For example, if a piece of dirt is worth $1 million today, you tell the vendor that you will give him $2 million on closing if you can have all the time you need to work on it; because if you are able to get all the rezoning, it's really worth $2 million; if you don't get the zoning, you don't close.

Once you agree on the timing and the price, then you should negotiate hard for the smallest possible non-refundable deposit, known as option money or earnest money.

If the deposit is subject to certain terms — and these terms vary with every deal — you can then put a larger deposit down knowing that the entire deposit is refundable up until the time you remove your conditions. If you have any revisions, extensions or changes to make, of course the time to make them is before you remove your conditions.

Another principle to remember when purchasing any project is that usually the most attractive and least expensive financing is an arrangement whereby the vendor provides financing for you to acquire the project, usually referred to as a vendor take-back mortgage. Although you may wonder why a vendor would accept a low deposit and the risk of financing the purchase, remember that you will never get what you don't ask for. Never assume what the seller will or will not accept. Make your offer on the basis that you want the best terms and conditions that you can get.

And finally, never remove the final-subject clause on an acquisition until at least your key adviser has inspected the prospective purchase. And your key adviser — your trusted second — should probably be a different person for each type of investment, depending upon the type of expertise you require. The only consistency is that the selected individuals must be people you trust absolutely, people who have your best interests at heart. They should be advisers whose judgement you do not question and who will, if necessary, confidently and quickly contradict you no matter how great the pressure is to go with a project or its terms. If I had followed this rule in the early eighties when the recession hit, I would never have lost $30 million.

I tend to become easily and almost irrevocably enthusiastic about a project before I know enough about it, and I shop around for opinions until I find someone who agrees with me. It can be pretty hard for my employees and advisers to stop the steam-roller of my enthusiasm and get me to examine the details. But they are smart, strong people who know that in the end, after I have finally listened to reason, it will be their job to go back to the other party and tell them that Peter has had a change of heart. It's a tough job but that's what my team is trained to do.

The point at which they do it is probably the most important part of the negotiating process. We've got eager, motivated dealers on both sides and an opposite party who can practically taste the done deal; then someone from my office comes in with reservations, questions, doubts. The decibel level of our enthusiasm begins to drop off sharply. The other party becomes anxious to save the deal, to negotiate; the terms offered us gradually get better and better, until I am reluctantly convinced to go through with the deal.

My style is always to say yes initially to any suggestion, and people often go away thinking I'm very easy to do business with. They may even think that I'm a knockover, or that the deal is done. But the object of being so agreeable is to get all of the information on a project that is necessary to make my final decision. People are much more forthcoming if they think they have an eager party. Armed with the complete picture, I can then start looking for the negative elements, and if there are enough of them, I start saying no.

Vendors are usually quick to sing the praises of an asset but are reluctant to dwell on the negative aspects of it at the outset. It is much like beginning a courtship: the relationship doesn't become viable until you get to know each other better.

I like to use salesmanship in negotiating a deal; it gets everyone cranked up. This isn't just a manipulative strategy — it is the way my mind works — enthusiasm followed by doubt followed by compromise.

That sort of tactic saves an awful lot of hard cash. It's called "working your way to no": you start out with "Yes, yes!" gather your data and gradually eliminate some or all of the yeses. I always try to leave the room saying, "Yes, but I'll have to send my people to have a look at it."

Sometimes I forget to qualify my enthusiasm. That's when my CEO, Eugene Kaulius, steps in to haul me out. A particularly painful example was my attempt to invest in a mortgage-brokerage firm in Ontario. In 1988 I went on a speaking tour and appeared before a gathering of brokers in a major city there. Afterwards, I went back to the offices of one firm that had a cash flow in the millions of dollars and got quite excited about what they were up to. I saw it as an opportunity to supply Century 21 salespeople with mortgage-financing services and I called Eugene all excited about it. He made arrangements to go to Ontario immediately and check it out. Before I left I came to an agreement in principle that, subject to our due diligence, we were going to invest.

Eugene flew into the city on a Saturday and immediately went into a meeting with the key executives of the firm. He spent a week there assessing it, and the more he saw the less he liked it. First, the firm was run on a basis that had worked in that city but would probably not work elsewhere. Also, it was a city that the major financial institutions had not yet saturated; when they did, the community would require the services of such brokers less and less — the banks would deal directly with investors and consumers. The advertising and marketing services provided would be progressively less and less in demand.

Secondly, the house was accepting investors' deposits that were being funnelled into land development, which was extremely risky. Thirdly, if the firm experienced any problems on the deposit side, the whole operation would be headed for disaster, since all its divisions were closely connected financially. Finally, the owner wanted a large cash payment to him directly rather than an investment in the company, which is what we felt the firm needed to flourish.

Eugene managed to extricate us from the deal and thereby saved my skin. The brokerage firm later experienced a reduction in deposit income and went belly-up.

My trusted advisers not only go in to deliver the bad news, they also move in if I inadvertently run over the tulips; they go back and stroke them and hold them up, look after them — in other words, they clean up after me. Public relations is especially important at those times when you let someone down on a deal; you don't want him to go away hating you or feeling humiliated or abused. In business it is essential to treat people as if today were their (and your) last day on Earth.

FIVE

Jumping Out the Window of Opportunity: The Sale of Century 21

Henry Chester said about the word
enthusiasm:

It's one of the greatest assets of man. It
beats money, power and influence. Single-
handedly enthusiasm tramples over
prejudices and opposition. It spurns
inaction and storms the citadel of its
object. Like an avalanche, it overwhelms
and engulfs all of its obstacles. It is
nothing more or less than faith in action.
The nice thing about enthusiasm is that it
is as contagious as the measles.
— Peter Thomas's Personal Goals
and Values Guide

In the late 1980s, at the same time that I was struggling with Heritage USA, I took a hard look at the economy. I had already lost my shirt once, and I could see
recession hitting again. I was sure that the situation
would worsen in the early 1990s.

I'd watched the revenue in Century 21 fluctuate,
and by 1988 it was the highest it had ever been. The
company was worth $50-$60 million. It was my opinion

that it would be several years before Century 21 Real Estate was worth that kind of money again.

I had wanted to extract cash from the company for a long time — to cash in at least some of my chips. As Victoria's *Monday Magazine* noted in 1982, I had been lucky enough to be in the right spot and ready to make my fortune "during the heady, speculative years of the 1970s, when the map of Canada seemed to lift up at its eastern power base, spilling population and pools of capital west." Then the recession had hit, Skalbania Enterprises had collapsed and my net worth had decreased by 50 percent in one year. That was $30 million — gone.

Although I managed to recoup, the lesson was never lost on me. I didn't want it to happen again. I recognized from first-hand experience how vulnerable I was to the vagaries of the economy over time, how easy it was to lose a fortune overnight.

As Sam Belzberg once told me, never fall in love with an asset; there is a time to buy and a time to sell.

There was also another critical reason it was time to sell in 1988: the tax laws were about to change. In 1989 there would be a major increase in capital gains included for calculating taxable income. By doing the deal before that, I saved $3 million net in taxes.

What's more, there was a lot of new competition coming into the marketplace. Some foreign brokers were moving in and competing so hard that they were reducing commissions and forcing others to do so — unheard-of in the Canadian industry. And new franchise schemes were appearing, offering similar services to real estate brokers at reduced fees. In some quarters, major Toronto brokers reported that less than half their salesmen were doing deals.

I am almost obsessed with my personal security in this world because I have seen so much go up in smoke. In Edmonton I saw major real estate operations like Jim Martin's Ithican Developments and Ken Rogers's Abacus Cities disappear. I watched Donald Cormie's Principal Group disappear. These were people I had learned from and done business with when I was just starting out. Nelson Skalbania and Peter Pocklington and more recently Robert Campeau — all of them started to fall in the 1980s. Fortunes were eroded. And I'm a Johnny-come-lately. It had taken me twenty years to come from nothing to where I was in the late 1980s, and I could see losing it all with the snap of a finger. I wanted my cash out so badly that I could taste it.

One thing that differentiates me from those players who went down is the fact that once I am financially secure, I don't feel I need to continue to make money for its own sake. Nor am I a workaholic who needs to do deals for their own sake — one of those men for whom the money is just the icing on the cake. These are lessons I learned through the bankruptcy of Skalbania Enterprises.

Although I learned a lot by observing men like Robert Campeau and successes like Jimmy Pattison and others, while I was studying them my motivations changed. I have developed new values and priorities over the years. Today my health, my family, travel and simply experiencing as much of life as I possibly can — these priorities have superseded my former ambitious, driven nature. As I noted earlier, when I look back, I wish that I had spent more time with my family when the kids were growing up.

I have no intention of dropping dead in my office. In 1988 I turned fifty years old and it was time to take stock and change direction. Age fifty is a good time to sell your deal. It is the perfect time to ensure your financial security for life and then get on with the other things that this world has to offer.

Consideration of other goals, values and priorities in addition to professional and financial success seems to be missing from business success books I have read. They tell readers how to get rich and climb to the top of the corporation, but they don't mention the toll it takes, or the other important factors in life besides wealth and power. Our society seems to be devoted to these two status symbols for their own sake, and simply getting more and more of both for some people is the whole purpose of being alive. Many of the cultural heroes of the 1980s were people like that — people like Donald Trump and Robert Campeau.

To me, it is important to be able to enjoy and benefit from the things that money can buy — and that includes the freedom to set work aside to get closer to my family, to look after my health through reduced stress, better diet, and exercise, and to dare to try new things, whether they be recreational or professional.

It is also important to be able to look at yourself in the mirror and say: I have made a contribution. For me that means involving myself in the government of the province I live in. I volunteered and was appointed to act as chairman of the British Columbia Housing Management Commission and the Privatization Review Committee. It is my conviction that we get the kind of government that we earn through personal participation. It is incumbent upon all of us at some time in our lives to get involved politically, whether it be at the grass roots level or running for office, in order to build the type of country we wish to live in.

All these considerations profoundly altered my attitude toward Century 21 Real Estate. I knew that my motivation was gone and I just didn't have the enthusiasm that allowed me to do the job as well as I'd done it in the past — as well as it should be done. That is the time to sell. My motivation to lead Century 21 was gone and I was driven instead by my desire for financial security. I felt it was time to bank some cash. I wanted to be a seller.

In 1987 I met with representatives of Midland Doherty, who found a group of investors who wanted to acquire a large interest in the company. They were going to take a debenture position but the debenture would only have been paid from profits, so it was a very good deal. Stu Henry, then Senior Vice-President and Director of Corporate Finance for Midland Doherty — and today on the board of Samoth Capital Corporation — had arranged a $15 million sale for part of my shares. Had that sale gone through, I would have pulled out 72 percent of $15 million. I would have had over $10 million in the bank all told and that would have been enough cash for me. With that nest egg, I'd gladly have held on to the rest of my shares.

But by the time Gary Charlwood agreed with my plan, the market crashed. I couldn't talk him into accepting the proposal quickly enough. I think that he was concerned about losing control of the company, especially if it went public later on — which is one of the options I was considering. In my opinion, Gary really didn't understand timing. By the time he had agreed to the concept, it was too late. The window of opportunity had passed and Black Monday of 1987 was upon us.

Finally I decided that the only way to extract myself from my relationship with Gary Charlwood was to trigger the buy-sell clause in our partnership agreement by making an offer to purchase Gary's shares, so that I could either sell the whole operation or a portion of it — but would no longer be frustrated in my attempt to cash in some chips. Alternatively he could buy me out, on the terms established in my offer. According to our shotgun buy-sell agreement, when one party offers to buy the other out, the latter either has to accept the offer or buy his partner's shares on the same terms. The party triggering the buy-sell clause sets the terms and conditions of the sale. On August 8, 1988, I pulled the trigger.

It was a win-win situation for me, whichever way it went. I very much wanted to take Century 21 public as a part of Samoth Capital — that was what my emotions dictated. But as I frequently do when making a major business decision, I contacted a few of my trusted business associates to ask them whether I should be a buyer or a seller. I outlined in writing the current status of the company, my partnership agreement with Gary Charlwood, and the company's position in the current economy. That information went in for-your-eyes-only confidence to several people, including Stu Henry and my lawyer for Samoth Capital in Toronto, Jack Gilbert. All advice came back to me with the same message: Sell.

As Nelson Skalbania put it to me in his inimitable if arguable fashion: "There are only two reasons to go public: either you're broke or you're stupid." As a general rule I don't agree, but in this case the Nelsonism applies.

What happened after that was an exercise in bluster and posturing that sharply increased the workloads of secretaries and the bank accounts of lawyers. Some people consider such things corporate intrigue; I consider most of it chicken droppings. It was a classic example of doing corporate battle: lining up the tanks on both sides in the hope that a few shots hit home. I made my offer to buy — an offer that may not, strictly speaking, have adhered to the terms of the buy-sell clause; but nobody took issue. Sure enough, Gary took the bait. On October 6, 1988, Gary gave notice that he rejected the offer and countered it with an offer to buy the company himself on the same terms as I had offered; the deal was to be closed in sixty days, on December 6. The battle lines were drawn.

Not long after Gary's offer, a Deep Throat came forward from within the staff at Century 21 headquarters to say that Gary had told them not to take any calls from me or to convey any information to me. What's more, the financial statements that always came from Gary on a regular basis became less frequent and less complete. Most seriously, I discovered indirectly that plans were afoot to diversify the company in ways that could have, in my opinion, seriously jeopardized profits and therefore my income from the management contract that was part of the deal: evidently Gary was considering moving into mortgages, life insurance and corporate relocation, as well as hiring a recruiter to expand franchise sales. Moreover, I was led to believe that perhaps standards for franchise prospects were being lowered to enhance sales.

In October 1988 I discovered that, on the instructions of someone at Century 21 Canada headquarters, a mailbag containing a letter that I had written to franchisees announcing the impending sale had not been sent out; instead it was hidden and loaded into the trunk of a car belonging to an official from head office.

And for reasons that are still beyond me, one board

member was tracked down in Africa by Gary's lawyer and told that the sale of Century 21 could not go through on December 6 unless all directors resigned, which he did; however, it came out later at the closing of the deal that the resignations were not necessary.

As a result of Gary's counter-offer, on October 13, 1988, the front page of the Toronto *Globe and Mail* "Report on Business" section had carried the headline: Thomas Loses Control in Century 21 Buyout. The story beneath the headline began, "Peter Thomas, who recently lost out in a bid to buy the bankrupt PTL ministry and its Heritage USA theme park, is also losing control of the real estate empire he founded." On the same day, the headline in the Vancouver *Province* blared: Thomas Gunned Down above a picture of Gary Charlwood holding a globe. The caption announced, "He's got the whole world in his hands."

Poor Peter, outsmarted again, this time by Gary Charlwood.

The fact was that the battle was far from over but I had already won the war. I never attempted to correct those stories, which were picked up and repeated in several publications. And the reason is an object lesson for all deal makers.

I never turned over my shares to Gary Charlwood at the closing and the sale was not completed on December 6, 1988. The upshot was that in March 1989 Gary Charlwood and Peter Thomas, after years of being thorns in each other's sides, faced off in the Supreme Court of British Columbia before Chief Justice Beverley McLachlin, later appointed to the Supreme Court of Canada.

My lawyers informed the court that we declined to close primarily because there was no proof that Gary Charlwood could write the necessary $25 million cheque to cover the $23 million purchase price and the interest due over the year he had to pay the money. The reality was that there was no money. According to the terms of the deal I was to turn my shares over for only $500,000 and a promissory note — those were the terms of the buy-sell clause in our original partnership agreement — and there was no proof that Gary could raise the $25 million needed for the final closing in a year's time. I'm sure that when they drew up the partnership agreement my legal advisers at the time had no idea what the company would be worth eventually.

Upon legal advice I took the position that I would not tender the shares until there was proof. That meant forcing Gary to take me to court if he wanted the sale to go through. It was my legal advice that in court he would have to show proof of ability to finance his purchase. As we expected, Gary sued.

Civil proceedings usually take years because the defendant puts every possible roadblock in the way to delay his day in court. But I was pushing this case through with the same urgency that Gary was. I wanted a done deal one way or the other, and I did nothing to stall it. Within three months of failure to close, we were in court. On April 11, 1989, Judge McLachlin issued her decision in favour of Gary Charlwood. I was "forced" to turn over my shares, accept $500,000 and a promissory note, and conclude the deal.

I sold my 72 percent share in Century 21 Real Estate of Canada to my partner Gary Charlwood and his financers, the Independent Order of Foresters, Sun Life Insurance Company, for $25 million plus a two-year management contract based on 54 percent of the profits. I also agreed to stay on as chairman of the board for a further two-year period. Altogether, the deal wasn't a bad return on my original $5,000 deposit.

The story on the street was that I tried to pull out of the deal at the last minute, was taken to court and lost. But you have to make sure that you don't let your ego ruin your deals. If you don't let the fear of what people think derail your strategy, you'll be laughing all the way to the bank. If you let bad press get to you emotionally, you're sunk. You never negotiate through the press. Besides, "bad press" can often, strategically speaking, be just exactly what you want.

And for three years after the sale, that is exactly what I wanted, because it was going to take me at least that long to ensure that I would get my disputed interest payments on the year-long $23 million "loan" and the balance of my management contract fees from Gary Charlwood. It was to my distinct advantage to appear to be the loser as I filled out my deposit slip at the bank.

In retrospect, I wouldn't have handled the sale the same way again, strategically speaking. Jack Gilbert, lawyer for and member of the board of my public company, Samoth Capital Corporation, advised me to be the one to sue Gary Charlwood to prove that he had the money to do the deal. Jack advised that the plaintiff always looks like the innocent party and the defendant like the guilty party in the public eye when it comes to lawsuits — particularly a lawsuit like this one, which in all likelihood would be settled with little or no time in court. That in fact was the image that stuck with us in media coverage of the case and I should have taken Jack's advice. If I had it to do over again, I would have handed the shares over to Gary and closed. If he did not fund on schedule then my alternative would have been to sue him.

Take the old adage about all publicity being good publicity and add to it a net worth of $23 million in cash after the sale was completed in 1989. What you get are two things: first, there are people pounding on your door every minute with deals, because they know you are worth that kind of cash — hey, it says so right here in the *Financial Post*; second, your life is totally, irrevocably, profoundly changed. That cash put me in a completely different world; I no longer have merely a net-worth statement that could change with tomorrow's closing stock-market report. Money doesn't mean the same to me as it does to most people anymore. It gives me an awesome freedom to do whatever I want with my life. I say to myself, "What's next?" and the options seem limitless.

On December 6, 1989, the principal amount of the promissory note, $23 million, was paid in full. The interest-payment dispute and the management agreement issues were resolved in an out-of-court settlement agreed to amicably by Gary and myself on December 7, 1990.

Today, my Century 21 money is my go-to-hell money. With it, I can live the life I want.

As I noted, the realization that I no longer had the enthusiasm to energize myself or my staff at Century 21 was key to my decision to sell. I believe the real secret of my success is my ability to attract, motivate and retain people who are better than I am, then motivate them to "dare to make more mistakes." It's amazing how, when you delegate to the right people, they rise to the task.

Most entrepreneurs share the same fatal flaw: they believe that they must be all things to all people — they must be able to do it all. They really don't believe that they need anybody and they are convinced that they can do the job — any job — better themselves.

I've always felt that Winston Churchill's image was created by the need at the time he came to power. He was just a short man who smoked cigars until there was a need for a saviour for England and he rose to the challenge. We all have the potential to be like that, to rise to the task at hand. I let my employees and associates know that I believe that and that they have been hired because they have skills I do not possess. I make it clear that I am not a manager or administrator, that I'm impatient with details and do not spend time on day-to-day operations; that's their job. If they have problems, they should let me know and I'll listen sympathetically and help strategize, but they have to work out the details. My role is to put good people in place and stay out of their way.

That philosophy brings out the best in people. Gradually, as they prove themselves, they can be given more and more opportunities to stretch their skills as more and more responsibilities are delegated. In effect, they are given a chance to fail, to test their limits.

Every month that you are in business you have to have a miracle worker. That is, every month each worker has to pull his or her own weight to cover overhead and contribute to profit. But one person has to perform a miracle — exceeding all the others in the coups he or she pulls off to improve the company. Appoint a different executive to be that employee each month, assigning them at the beginning of the year. During that month the employee has to bring in one-twelfth of the profit of the company for the year. The effort to do so builds a great esprit de corps and enhances each person's feeling of accomplishment when he or she pulls off the miracle.

You should also establish a consistent form of recognition for those times when the miracle worker succeeds — a reward system like my gold AMC pins and monetary bonuses. And leave your door open for staff to come to you with anything that is on their minds; often you will not want to deal with all their concerns yourself, but you should make sure that someone else in the operation does.

Enthusiasm is the critical factor in motivating people. "Infectious enthusiasm" is a phrase often used in print to describe my style. What these commentators are saying is that I'm a good salesman — of myself and of my vision. It is important to be able to get staff excited about their role in your business or your latest venture. If you are good at getting people to respect you, they will want to work with you and be loyal to you and perform their best for you. They must feel confident in your sincerity and your genuine enthusiasm about them. People have to believe that you care, are totally committed to your cause and that you respect them, in order for that caring and commitment to be returned.

Infusing your sphere of influence with energy and genuine enthusiasm is important not just for your employees, but for everyone you interact with. If people come to me with new ventures that have potential, a little energy and enthusiasm can motivate them to go away and do their homework and come back with an even better version of the same thing. You don't tell such people that they haven't thought the project through: you show them that you are keen and ask a few pointed questions, and sooner or later you will probably have a doable deal. You can motivate people to buy what you are selling, to sell on your terms what you want to buy, to work for you and perform well, or to see the wisdom of quitting. It really is all up to you.

It is important to let your people know that you think they are up to the task — even if they have never done such a thing before. You can demonstrate the conviction that people can rise to a challenge if only they have the will. Seemingly insurmountable problems can be overcome if that will is invoked and guided. One way that I motivate those around me is to share the sentiments in this regard that I have collected over the years in my Personal Goals and Values Guide.

PETER THOMAS'S TEN INSPIRATIONAL MOTIVATORS

1. *There are people who've got what it takes to make it happen; there are people who have worked very hard to make it happen; and there are people who say, "What happened?"*

There is an old story that is part of American folklore — I have no idea if it is true — about an immigrant who wanted to improve his lot in life. He applied for a job as a garbageman and his new employer gave him a card listing the places where he had to collect the garbage. When the immigrant simply stood there staring at the card, the employer realized that his new employee couldn't read and fired him on the spot. Realizing the man was hungry, the employer gave him a bunch of bananas when he sent him on his way.

The immigrant took the bananas and sat down on a park bench to think about his predicament. Someone came along and asked him if he could buy one of his bananas. The immigrant sold him one for a nickel; an hour later he had sold all the bananas for fifty cents. He took that fifty cents and went back and bought an even bigger bunch of bananas and went through the same process all over again.

Eventually the man became a street vendor. Then he saved enough money to buy a fruit store and then another fruit store.

The former beggar eventually became very rich. When he retired and sold his company he sat down with his lawyer to prepare the papers for the sale. When the lawyer handed him the agreement to review and sign, he just looked at it quizzically.

The lawyer asked, "Well, aren't you going to read it?"

"Sir, I cannot read," he answered simply.

The lawyer sat back, stunned. "Do you realize, sir, what a successful man like you could have been if only you had learned to read?"

"Yes," he replied, "I could have been a garbageman."

2. *Confucius said: "He who tries something and fails is infinitely greater than he who tries nothing and succeeds."*

There have been enterprises I have undertaken that

have failed — Triexcellence car dealerships and Mr. Build franchises to name only two.

In the case of Triexcellence, the timing of the concept was wrong. With Mr. Build, the concept was fine and the timing was good, but there was no main motivator who had both his cash and reputation on the line in the deal. I wasn't interested in doing all over again what I had done once already with Century 21 — I wanted to go on to different, bigger things. That's what I should have done instead of taking this project on myself.

In both cases, these franchise schemes — both of which were the brainchildren of Century 21's founder, Art Bartlett — had not achieved the same market penetration across the border as Century 21 Real Estate had when I bought that scheme. The world wasn't ready for these ideas because it had had very little exposure to them and we couldn't point to a proven success rate. In retrospect, I think I jumped on Art Bartlett's bandwagon too quickly.

I also learned from these experiences to stay away from businesses I did not know inside out. Selling skills alone are not good enough and I couldn't trade simply on the track record of Century 21. If I had to do it again, I would let Art build up the U.S. trade and perfect the business before I jumped in.

3. *Make no small plans, for they have no magic to stir our souls; great ideas attract great people.*

This quote comes from James J. Hill, president of the Great Northern Railroad. By doing exciting and challenging things, you create energy within yourself and among those around you. Things happen that might otherwise not have happened without that energy. It's contagious. It creates adrenaline that functions like gasoline — you run on it. You don't eat much, you don't sleep because you're on a high.

When things are going wrong or you are feeling lethargic you see the opposite effect: that negative energy starts moving you and your world in reverse. That's because there's no action and your inaction leaves you time to read the paper all morning — which is often full of negative news; you have time to listen to the grievances of your friends who are in trouble, which is negative; and you've got time to be bombarded by the real world.

When you are operating with a goal and are motivated and active, you don't focus on the negatives in the real world; instead, you focus on the positives. If you are totally focused on where you are going, you are not affected as much by negative elements. The glass is always half-full rather than half-empty.

4. *Not having a goal is more to be feared than not reaching a goal.*

When you set a goal, tell others about it. You are more likely to stick to it if you think others will see you fail. Tell the whole world: your friends, your bankers, your spouse — whoever will listen to you — about what you are going to do. The more people you tell the more committed you become to the goal yourself. You will plan step-by-step the way you are going to achieve that goal. Whether it is running a marathon or building a multimillion-dollar company, each goal is a journey that begins with that first step.

Never be afraid to fail — think of your failures as object lessons. Eddy Arcaro, perhaps the greatest jockey who ever rode a horse, sat on 250 losers before he rode his first winner.

5. *Not only do you need the will to win, you also need the will to prepare to win.*

Positive thinking alone will not guarantee success. The right attitude includes the conviction that you need to be prepared. Do all your homework before you undertake completion of your task; get all the help you need and make sure you go back and get more time if you need it to do the job right. Know what you don't know. Learn to be a streetwise strategic thinker.

6. *My attitude is my choice; I can't change the world or my surroundings but I can change my attitude about them.*

When Nelson Skalbania restructured his finances, my attitude was that it was not going to suck me under. I decided to fight: I was not going into bankruptcy. Once I had taken the attitude that I wasn't going to be a loser, I structured myself to win. I put Eugene Kaulius in charge of the lawsuits, sent my army helmet over to my lead lawyer, John Norton, and went about devoting my time exclusively to making money and focusing on the positives in my world — things like my health, my freedom and my happiness.

7. *Some men die by shrapnel,*
   Some go down in flames,
   But most men perish inch by inch,
   Playing at little games.

   Remember that work expands to fill the time allotted for it. Beware of such time wasters as going into the office because that is where you are expected to be; calling and/or attending unnecessary meetings; and analyzing deals you most likely will not do. Handle a piece of paper only once. Review your plans for the next day each evening to ensure that you do not become a robot trapped into a preprogrammed schedule.

8. *Kahlil Gibran said that "our greatest joys spring forth from the same well that held our greatest sorrows."*

   World War II and the loss of my father in a peculiar way led to the luckiest event of my life: immigration to Canada. Without that, I believe that none of the achievements that have brought me to where I am today would have been possible.

9. *Today is going to be the best day of my life.*

   I had to repeat this little quote to myself like a mantra when I was fighting to avoid bankruptcy. If you tell yourself this each day when you rise, and mean it, your personal performance and the per-

NEVER FIGHT WITH A PIG

formance of those around you will be enhanced miraculously. We never exceed our expectations of ourselves and our expectations are contagious.

10. *Don't wait for extraordinary opportunities; seize common occasions and make them great.*

Leaving a beach in Hawaii to hop on a plane to California and check out a crazy real-estate-franchising scheme was the best use of a common occasion that I have ever made. It ruined my suntan but if I had waited until the conference was over, or taken the time to check things out slowly first, someone else might have had the Century 21 franchise for Canada.

The best pointers in my Personal Goals and Values Guide, however, are those I reserve for myself, as guidance in motivating others.

1. *It is amazing what you can do if you don't care who gets the credit.*

With Gary Charlwood getting all the credit for the success of Century 21, I was able to put $23 million in the bank.

2. *What you send out is sent back to you.*

Your positive vibes, respect, confidence and enthusiasm will generate a response in kind from others. The same is true of negativity, abuse and sham. You will motivate in others the sentiments and behaviour you demonstrate.

3. *Promise a lot and give more.*

My employees and associates are motivated by the material benefits, promotions, recognition and prestige I promise for good performance, but I always promise a little less than I actually plan to reward them with. There are always surprise bonuses, many for no obvious reason except to show my appreciation and stimulate higher levels of motivation. Wealth affords you the privilege of displaying generosity and that privilege should be treasured; but even the not-so-wealthy can find little ways to show they care. It always pays off.

One working day I took all the staff of our head office out to a speedway where they took a speed-driving course, piloting their own cars around the racetrack. Another time I took them all sky-diving; after a brief instruction period, they all took a sky-dive. Each summer we go out on my boat across Georgia Strait for a company picnic.

4. *The people are more important than the project.*

Entrepreneurs must attract achievers. This is especially true when you are considering a new venture that includes people in the package. If you don't have a good feeling about the people, don't do the project — no matter how attractive it might look. And if you try to cut corners on salaries or staff to keep your budget in line, it is a false economy. Put on your strategic thinking cap and decide exactly what you need by way of personnel and get it. Then motivate loyalty among these people so they will stick with you and perform well for you.

Conversely, watch for the weak link in the chain and set specific, reasonable goals for that person; motivate him or her to achieve them. Monitor that person and assist him or her in overcoming their hurdles. If the goals are not reached, sooner or later that worker will see the wisdom of finding another job better suited to his or her skills. Either fire them up with enthusiasm or fire them out with enthusiasm.

Whether you are interviewing potential employees or considering a new venture, go with your gut. If your instinct tells you that you are less than totally comfortable with someone, don't get involved with that person.

5. *Pay slightly above-average salaries and even higher bonuses.*

Bonuses encourage peak performance and attract people who are hard-driving, ambitious and competitive. Those who would choose a high salary with no bonus system are likely to be poor performers. What you want is people who have a constant need to prove themselves to themselves, no matter what the level of achievement. Bonuses give people a chance to do that and high bonuses reward it. You need to find people who enjoy this system of rewards.

6. *Your job requires selling yourself and dealing with others as if they were family and friends, not pieces of meat.*

In the same way that you must see a prospective

purchaser through his own eyes before you will be
able to make a sale, you must see your staff and
associates from their point of view before you can
stimulate peak performance. The camaraderie of
your office is critical: you need a team that is pulling together, not individuals immersed in their
own political agendas and personal problems. Your
job is to bring them out of their private worlds into
the larger one of your operation and you can only
accomplish that if you convince them of your sin-
cere concern for their best interests.

You can feel the atmosphere of any office as soon as
you walk into it, and you know whether that atmosphere is healthy or not. You know how much
energy is being devoted to self-serving, petty office
politics. You know right away how much people
are enjoying what they do and how efficiently and
enthusiastically they are doing it. Your aim should
be to make sure your office feels good for others to
walk into and you do that by selling yourself just
the way you would sell a product or piece of
property.

7. *Be a born-again business person: sell your vision with
evangelistic fervor. Sell your concept as if your life
depended on it. Your conviction will be contagious.*

A couple of years ago the *Globe and Mail* "Report on
Business" said that my religion is optimism and
that I preach "the gospel of salesmanship around
the world." Anyone who has attended one of my
motivational seminars or viewed one of my tapes
will be aware of the fact that my style does have a lot

in common with an evangelist's and that's deliberate. Although the approach is more subdued in the office and around the negotiating table, it draws converts like a magnet.

8. *Preach the gospel of Attitude, Motivation and Commitment.*

The concept of giving top achievers a gold AMC pin arose when I was trying to come up with ways to motivate my Century 21 franchisees. An author friend of mine came to me with his book and suggested I use it as a bonus gift to them. When I read it I realized that it wasn't something that they would like at all. But I liked the idea of giving a gift. So I decided to create something myself; the problem was what to give them.

I was preparing an upcoming talk on the kinds of things you need to be successful, and developed a long list. When I tried to cut it down I realized that everything on the list fit into three categories — attitude, motivation and commitment. With the right mix of these three elements, you will not only be rich, you will be happy because you will do nothing unless you have a positive attitude toward it, are highly motivated to do it and are totally committed to it.

When others see that in you the word spreads fast — suddenly everyone wants to do business with you. First they watched you sell your way in the door, then they watched you get the job done up to expectations or maybe better, much better — and you're off! Now everyone knows you are not a disappearing salesman. That's the real estate term for someone who performs like a well-trained seal, promising you anything in order to get your listing, and then disappears — he or she only shows up again to renew the listing.

It's important to take on only assignments or projects that you enjoy; you won't perform well at those you don't enjoy. The money you will make is not enough of a motivation to guarantee success because the attitude and commitment just aren't there.

9. *Use the twelve most persuasive words in the English language: you, money, save, new, results, health, easy, safety, love, discover, proven and guarantee.*

According to a Yale University study, the two most important words are: Thank you. The three most influential three-word phrases are: Will you please? Could I help? I love you. The last word another person wants to hear is: I.

10. *Do your best to dispel fear, uncertainty and doubt. This is just one more aspect of the evangelistic salesman's job.*

One of the reasons some people don't achieve a lot in life is the disease called FUD: Fear, Uncertainty and Doubt. If you wait until you know everything about something, you'll never do it. You cannot pinpoint all the risks in advance and you cannot prevent all mistakes. You must embark upon a goal even when you don't have all the answers or a guarantee that you will achieve it.

Many entrepreneurs go bankrupt because they don't have the time or the resources to do the necessary research. You do have to find a way to do that research or you shouldn't take on the project; but you can't expect to have a crystal ball that will remove all doubt and uncertainty. You simply have to overcome the fear they can sometimes engender. Do most of your homework and then use your common sense. You'll be right more often than you will be wrong.

As a manager, you have to find people's comfort zone and massage it, stimulating feelings of security and relief from anxiety. You can pull people up to a level of peak performance only if they are not harbouring fears — of failure, of incurring your displeasure or of losing prestige or their jobs. That means building not only their self-esteem but also their faith in the stability and future of your company.

The motivational principles outlined here can be applied anywhere outside the workplace if you think of yourself as a catalyst. Decide on the qualities, skills and experience required of the people you need for a specific challenge. Attract the right people and ask them to work toward a common stated objective. Stimulate them to work as a team to produce ideas for achieving that objective within a specific time frame. I did this as chairman of the British Columbia Housing Management Commission but you could use the same strategy to win a sailing race, raise funds for charity or renovate your home.

In every case, you must sell yourself as motivator and leader to those you wish to have cooperate with you. In the case of the Housing Management Commission, when my appointment and call for volunteers was announced, the *Financial Post* headed the story with the lead line: "My single-parent mom worked." Everybody knew about my success with Century 21, but I wanted to make sure that they knew that I appreciated the housing concerns of the average person, that I remembered my roots and sympathized with their problems. I've never forgotten my beginnings as a nanny's son who was born in England and grew up in rural Alberta, and I visit the old homestead site regularly to make sure I don't forget. In combination with my success in real estate, that makes me more than just another millionaire developer, it makes me the right man for the job at the Housing Commission, a person who, because of his background, could attract other appropriate people.

Be an optimist, but not naively so. Just keep pushing and stay upbeat. There are a million ways to solve a problem. It is a running joke among my friends and family — not to mention those who work for me — that I have amnesia when it comes to bad news. I can be dismissive when it is delivered and have total loss of recall immediately thereafter. Whatever the shortcomings of such an attitude, it certainly serves to motivate me and those around me to keep our spirits and efforts up.

The critics who read this will probably say this is shallow thinking and unrealistic. Remember I *choose* to focus on the positive. It does not mean I am not aware of the negative or I do not plan for the negative; it means that by focusing my energy on the positive aspects of any situation, it helps to overcome any hurdles put in my way.

This philosophy also relates to one's health, personal life and the day-to-day challenges that greet us each morning.

While you are busy motivating others, who is motivating you? You are. You do it first of all by reading positive, inspirational books and articles. The best print motivator I have is my Personal Goals and Values Guide. In addition to the inspirational motivators collected in it, I also list my wins over the years — things that have made me happy, given me a thrill, or simply things I have achieved in my business life.

Too many times we focus on negative experiences and losses, but if you can focus on positive experiences — the day you hit your first home run, for instance — then you will be motivated to go forward with gusto. When you are in a down mood and you are losing, stop and visualize that positive experience from your past when you were winning. Think of the crack of the ball hitting the bat, think of the yelling of the crowd, think of the dust, of the running to first, then second, then third and finally sliding victoriously all the way home. If you can visualize that in your mind, it is hard to lose the feeling of being a winner. The recollection of that will fill you full of enthusiasm and adrenaline that will get you out of your negative state of mind. Many times when I feel that I need to be motivated, I've made a list of my past wins to pump me up to meet the next challenge. I take a peek at my list of wins in the Goals and Values Guide every day. I read the whole thing every week and I am constantly adding to it.

I recommend that everyone create his or her own personal guide and do the same. Revise and update your guide annually. Mine is divided into the following sections. Each section includes inspirational passages I have gleaned from my reading.

1. *Goals, Values and Philosophies*

    This section includes a review of the previous year's highlights under three categories: health, happiness and freedom as well as a list of that year's major business projects, a list of the fun times I've had over the past year and a list of my values and priorities and what steps I will take this year to further them. These include everything from health and weight control to goals for reading, watching television (only planned television allowed) and drinking (no alcohol, only one cappuccino per day) and communication with my various enterprises.

    In 1989 I resolved to take one weekday off a week; on that day I do anything and everything other than work. Last year I resolved never to pass on rumour, innuendo or hearsay, nor criticize, condemn or complain. Every year, resolve to do specific things to give you happiness, making a point of spoiling both yourself and your friends and family. Each year I list what I plan to do to increase my freedom.

    Next, this section lists all of the things that I have done during my life that have made me happy, made me proud, made me excited or were just a natural high. Then I list things I want to consider doing in the future that will do the same, breaking out some of them for the current year.

2. *Business Ground Rules and Speech Themes*

The business ground rules form the basis of *Never Fight With a Pig* and are divided into operational, philosophical, motivational and general rules. The speech themes expand upon these rules. I have assembled a list of the rules I have used over the years to guide my business and added those gained from books, workshops and mentors. In yours, you should make sure you jot down speech themes that occur to you in passing and transfer them to the guide annually.

3. *Humorous Business Anecdotes*

These keep my spirits up and assist me in keeping other people's up as well. They are complemented by a list of one-line bits of wisdom and observations that serve the same purpose. Your business will provide many others that are perhaps more appropriate for you and your co-workers.

4. *Humorous Anecdotes for Any Occasion*

These reflect my personal philosophy and are useful any time that I'm selling myself to people, whether in a formal speech, a sales presentation or casual encounter. Some of them appear in these pages. Make a habit of collecting your own.

5. *Joint Venture Partners*

This section provides vital statistics on my closest business associates and reminds me to review business matters with them and maintain communication on a regular basis.

6. *Financial Statements and Detailed Net Worth Statements by Assets*

    It is important to review these regularly to keep the master plan in mind and to examine both present position and the future course of action.

One of my favourite anecdotes in the Goals and Values Guide is one I like to contemplate whenever I am tempted to go into my attack mode. It is a story I heard Texas computer entrepreneur and multimillionaire extraordinaire Ross Perot tell about his childhood — a story that has guided his life to this day. Evidently when he was small, tramps kept coming to his mother's door, begging for food. One day Ross overheard a tramp ask his mother if they got more than their share of beggars at the house. She thought a moment and said that, come to think of it, she supposed she got more requests for handouts than anyone else in the neighbourhood.

The tramp asked her to step outside. He showed her a mark scratched into the sidewalk in front of the house; it was the vagabonds' code indicating that the people here were generous. The tramp offered to remove it to save her further harassment. Ross watched in silence as his mother stopped the tramp and insisted, "No, leave the mark there."

If someone else obviously thinks of you as "a mark," your response to that person is the true test of your character. It is important not to make your adversary's problem your own.

SIX

wn as the Wall of
mementos of my
ything from my
to recent shots
nd soloing in a

d platinum discs
stor behind The
ale *a cappella* pop
backer of a musi-

business associ-
under the Bank-
is he describes it,
lion in the hole, I
es to keep myself
bered that I had
ter Milborne, one
inium marketers,
led him to ask for

my money, but he said he didn't have it — the recession had been hard on him, too. What he did have, however, was a $25,000 management agreement from four singers who called themselves The Nylons; he said I could have that.

I had never heard of The Nylons. Hunter told me that their manager would get in touch to tell me more about them.

Not long afterwards I received a phone call from Toronto from Wayne Thompson, the manager, mentor and financial acumen behind the group. Wayne was an open and honest man and a true believer in the group's future. From that first conversation to the present day, Wayne remains The Nylons' best fan. He told me up front that I wasn't going to get my money back immediately, but he couched it in terms that made it seem like a marvellous opportunity to break into the entertainment industry.

It turned out that not only were The Nylons unable to pay, they also desperately needed $75,000 right away to keep themselves afloat. They were about to make their first push into the American market, and they required what is known in the industry as "tour support," to finance their first U.S. tour promoting their new album.

I thought about it and investigated the group. My two grown kids, Todd and Liane, knew about them and thought they were terrific. It turned out that The Nylons were a very impressive, original bunch who were on their way up.

I figured that if they didn't get that money, I would never see mine. Besides, being a producer of some glamorous young rising stars would be a real thrill. What's more, I needed an exciting new project to throw myself into while the sky was falling at Skalbania Enterprises. It was just what the doctor ordered: a mental tonic that allowed me to turn a negative experience into a positive one.

Wayne showed up in my Vancouver office. He turned out to be a tall, dark, lanky young man with a lot of style. We hit it off right away.

Finally I explained to him, "Look, I do two kinds of business: real estate deals for money, and other deals for fun. This one is definitely fun. I'll do it."

I scraped together the money for them from my Century 21 income. And later I gave them more money. Today The Nylons are wildly successful and by 1990 they had paid me back handsomely. They've progressed from a local Toronto cabaret act to a national concert act and finally to stardom in the international arena. Eighty-five percent of their income is from the U.S. market. Most of their time is spent performing out of the country, and we have gone on to negotiate a whole new deal for financial backing on a larger scale.

I often act as a mentor to members of the group. Arnold Robinson, the black bass singer, is a fun-loving individual who is always up, in spite of the fact that he's gone through three divorces. Claude Morrison, known as "the cute little one," is interested in personal investing and is curious about what's going on in the world around him. Paul Cooper was known as the creative member, but all of them "wrote" (that is, recorded on tape) and arranged their material. Paul left the group and was replaced by Micah Barnes. The late Marc Connors — the curly-headed blond — was the gregarious leader who had a good head for business. After his untimely death, Juno Award-winner Billy Newton-Davis joined the group.

When I talk to them, these men seem like four ordinary guys. But when they are together on stage, as soon as the lights go on they're totally transformed — they become larger than life. A magic aura surrounds them that makes them a very exciting act to watch — they put out a huge amount of energy. Not very many acts have that quality. It always thrills me, and I never tire of hearing them. But you'd never guess that they were this way if you met them on the street.

The basis of our relationship is the fact that I know Wayne Thompson is always being straight with me, and I am always straight with him. If that is the way people operate, I will do business with them. When money is the predominant issue, people's loyalties will often wane; that's when they show their true colours. At those times it's important to be the person who looks at other factors in the equation and makes the right choice, regardless of the money owed. I had to play that role when there were hostilities among the early investors in The Nylons; one of them wanted to get rid of Wayne, so I bought the investor out.

Over my eight-year association with The Nylons, there have been euphoric highs like successful foreign tours and seemingly bottomless lows when it looked as if there wasn't going to be enough money to keep going. Sometimes Wayne has had to come to me with very tough business news; often, he just couldn't pay what the group owed me. At those times I'd remind him that I'd made millions and lost millions and that this setback was just temporary, part of a cycle. I was confident that they would get their act together with the right kind of support. Inspiration is a better motivator than intimidation.

Looking back on it, this was perhaps my first

attempt to be a mentor outside my own realm. I cautioned Wayne that people like winners, and like to be associated with them. It's important to look and act like a winner at all times, no matter how rough life gets. It motivates staff and attracts good business. I know I was only confirming the positive aspects of Wayne's personality; we all need others to affirm our instincts.

I also advised him never to make a deal just for the sake of generating income: always keep career goals in mind. Don't make a deal simply because there is no money, especially if the deal impinges on basic principles and future direction. In the case of The Nylons, early in their career they stopped doing local clubs in order to make a record and undertake their thrust into the United States. Often they needed the money the clubs would bring in, but they knew that time and money spent on a U.S. tour or in the recording studio would be more fruitful in the long run.

It was Wayne's leadership that led them to make the right decisions about how to spend their time. Investors were pushing them to get on the Canadian club circuit and start generating cash flow rather than accumulating more debt on an expensive U.S. tour and recording-studio time, but The Nylons resisted the pressure, and their instincts proved right.

It took a lot of strength to stand up to the other four investors and mounting debts, and I encouraged that. I told them never to let people intimidate them — and don't be cajoled or lulled — into veering off a chosen career track. Too many people never achieve their dreams because they are forever caught up in meeting their immediate necessities. It's amazing how little money you can get by on if you have to, as Donna and I did in the early years.

When you are an entrepreneurial investor, it is important to be more than just a source of money; you have to be a source of smart money. I try hard to provide advice, energy, guidance and blessings, to be a driving force — to provide more than the value of the money alone. While sharing my hard-earned wisdom makes me feel needed, I also protect my investment by convincing my partners to increase their own financial stake in ventures; people always look after money better when it is their own.

Beyond the gratification of mentoring the group through the good times and the bad to eventual success, there are many perks for me in my relationship with The Nylons — that's what this kind of fun investment is all about. Wherever they perform, Wayne can get me or my friends in that town front-row seats to concerts — not just for their appearances, but for Madonna or anyone else. However, what we have done best together is have a good time all over the world: Las Vegas, Los Angeles, the Bahamas and Australia, for instance.

A few years ago The Nylons were going to Australia to be on the entertainment roster at the America's Cup race, and I arranged to do some motivational speaking there at the same time. We watched the race from the deck of *The Pacific Princess*, also known as *The Love Boat*, where I was giving my seminars. When we went on to their gigs in Brisbane and Perth, we went to parties, shows and dinner together. We mostly enjoyed relaxing and talking. Their performances were fantastic — they were very popular with the local crowds, who went crazy with cheers and applause as soon as The Nylons were announced.

When the group came to Vancouver for Expo 86, I handed Wayne the keys to my brand-new Rolls-Royce

180

convertible and told him it was theirs for the duration. I don't know who was more thrilled, Wayne or myself.

It is as important to me to do deals that provide thrills like that as it is to do multimillion-dollar projects. I divide my money equally between no-risk and high-risk investments and one of the deciding factors in selecting a high-risk investment is how much fun it is: how much Peter Thomas gets a kick out of the company he is keeping, and how much of an escape they provide. For a deal to be attractive it has to include interesting people I'd never have access to otherwise. Through making an investment in The Nylons, I had the opportunity to have one-on-one contact with a group of creative people in the world of show business that I would otherwise only read about in the paper. The investment provided a unique new experience, and that's what life is all about.

Among my experiences are climbing the pyramids of Egypt, rafting the Green River, climbing the Sugarloaf in Rio, going through the Panama Canal in the Love Boat, riding the Machu Picchu choo-choo, crossing Alligator Alley in Florida on a jet boat, running the New York Marathon at age forty-three, flying from Paris to New York on the Concorde in 1982, eating the fruits and vegetables of Tahiti, driving a Formula Ford race car at Sears Point International Raceway, attending the America's Cup race and the Cannes Film Festival, diving to 850 feet off the Cayman Islands in a submarine, scuba diving on the Great Barrier Reef and sky-diving at Abbotsford — not to mention travelling all over the world. That doesn't include my toy collection: cars, motorcycles, boats and planes.

Most of these recreational experiences are relatively recent, and they are the result of a profound change in the way I operate. My professional experiences have taught me a lot that has changed my views about what is important in life. I not only do business differently now, I also live my entire life differently.

SIX LESSONS I LEARNED THE HARD WAY

My little debacle with Nelson Skalbania taught me how important it was to stick to my principles and learn from my experiences. Deviation from them created the risk of falling victim to the following pitfalls and ultimately losing everything.

1. *Beware of the King Arthur Syndrome.*

    You are not infallible and you are not an expert on all things. Keep telling yourself this whenever you see everything you touch turning to gold. Otherwise you are in for a very humbling experience. It's hard to tell someone who has just made a million dollars that he is wrong about something, especially when he has been told the same thing before and made a fortune when he ignored the advice.

    You are falling victim to the syndrome if your deals are becoming so risky that you quit discussing them with your advisers and your spouse.

    One time I was in Eugene, Oregon, because my daughter, Liane, was attending a gymnastics meet. I had nothing to do so I bought a building called the Atrium for $1.4 million. I quickly sold it for $2.4 million. After that I was sure I was invincible and I never listened to anybody — right up until the time I had to hire John Norton to bail me out.

When you don't want to talk to anyone else, use your spouse as a listening post. Remember that you usually want to believe in the people you are dealing with for business reasons and are blind to their obvious personal shortcomings.

2. *Control your ego.*

    Ambition and greed can be your downfall. Set limits on the amount of money and power you want or you may end up with nothing. Don't be a workaholic who does deals for their own sake and don't abandon other goals and values in your effort to accumulate wealth mindlessly. How much money do you really need?

3. *Don't neglect management while you are focusing on acquisition.*

    Make sure that you personally see any new venture through the critical start-up phase before you delegate the bulk of the responsibility. I was the entrepreneur who made my first ventures work and no one else could do it for me later.

    Businesses I started that were not as successful as Century 21 failed in large part because I delegated the start-up and didn't throw myself into it. Delegation should have come later when start-up was complete and the operations had their own momentum.

4. *If you recognize a business cycle changing, don't feed a bad deal — cut your losses.*

Your heart and your head tend to follow where your cash went. There is no use fishing where there are no fish — there is a time to fish and a time to cut bait.

In the case of businesses that are floundering, you should establish a budget and set a realistic target date for certain specified results. Call on your key men and women to be accountable for certain goals by that date. If those goals aren't reached — after you've really thought about it — you cut; or you deliberately decide to extend the deadline for three months. At the point when you make that decision, you're no longer just feeding the deal and forgetting about it. Every three months you should reassess.

That is exactly what we did in the case of a franchise scheme I picked up from Art Bartlett called Mr. Build, which offers home repairs and renovations of all kinds under one umbrella company. The concept is a good one but I did not devote enough of my personal time to making it work.

5. *The only projects you should persist in are the ones wherein if you lose, you will lose small and if you win, you will win big.*

Never invest if there is a possibility that you can lose big, even if it is also possible to win big in the deal.

6.   *Don't blame the other guy.*

Any trouble I got into, I got into on my own. The
adrenaline rush I got from being on the edge was
addictive. It's a sickness. Soon I needed it — I
needed the feeling of gambling and not knowing
whether I was right or wrong. It becomes compul-
sive. Most people who have the King Arthur Syndrome would never think of gambling in Las Vegas
but they'll gamble in business. It's really the same
syndrome — they keep going to the table with bigger and bigger chips when any sensible person
would at least have taken some of their chips off the
table.

I still like the adrenaline rush but I limit it now in
business and redirect it toward my toys. I love cars
and boats and the outdoors. When I'm getting too
heavily immersed in business, I go out for a ride on
my mountain bike or my power boat. It keeps me
out of trouble. Dip into your toybox when you are
tempted to gamble too much in business.

The PHT Factor

Ultimately, what I consider the critical factor in any deal
is the PHT factor — myself. Never forget that you are the
most important part of any deal. That factor contributed
to my emotional distance from Heritage USA in the
end. I was nearly fifty years old, healthy and wealthy —
why did I need the aggravation of pulling this property
together? It was going to require a major commitment of
time and energy for an indefinite period of time on the

other side of the continent and it wasn't worth it. I could perhaps ruin my health or my private life in the attempt. I didn't need to do it just for the experience — life has too much else to offer.

I would like to close with a favourite story I included in my Personal Goals and Values Guide:

Remember the four-minute mile? People had been trying to achieve it since the days of ancient Greece. In fact, folklore has it that the Greeks had lions chase the runners, thinking that would make them run faster. They also tried tiger's milk — not the stuff you get down at the health-food store, the real thing. Nothing worked. So they decided it was impossible. And for over a thousand years everyone believed it. It was physiologically impossible for a human being to run a mile in four minutes. Our bone structure was all wrong. Wind resistance too great. Inadequate lung power. There were a million reasons.

Then one man, one single human being, proved that the doctors, the trainers, the athletes and the millions before him who had tried and failed were all wrong. And miracle of miracles, the year after Roger Bannister broke the four-minute mile, two other runners broke the four-minute mile and the year after that three runners broke the four-minute mile.

A few years ago, in New York, I stood at the finish line of the Fifth Avenue Mile and watched thirteen out of thirteen runners break the four-minute mile in a single race. In other words, the runner who finished dead last would have been regarded as having accomplished the impossible a few decades ago.

What happened? There were no great breakthroughs in training. Human bone structure didn't suddenly improve. But human attitudes did. You can accomplish your goals... if you set them. Who says you're not tougher, smarter, better, harder-working, more able than your competition? It doesn't matter if other people say you can't do it. The only thing that matters is whether or not you say it. Until Bannister came along, we all believed in the experts. Bannister believed in himself... and changed the world. If you can believe in yourself, well then, there's nothing you can't accomplish. So don't quit. Don't ever quit.

APPENDIX

Implementing Excellence

THE IMPORTANCE OF EXCELLENCE

During the recessionary early eighties, many business people marketed motivational seminars to counter the prevailing negativity and I was one of them. We all saw an opportunity to help others by spreading some of our energy and enthusiasm. "Implementing Excellence" was intended to help the business world get back on its feet, but it can be used by anyone who is striving for business success.

The first thing to remember is that your power to succeed is a function of your own personal perception. If you think you can, you can. The power is within you, the individual, and cannot come from someone else — your boss or your family or whoever else you might think controls your life or must give you a helping hand. Ultimately, they do not have the power that you have inside yourself to help you realize your dreams. Do you really know your own potential, or do you stay within the safety nets you have built for yourself, afraid to test your limits? Do you give up in the face of defeat or failure, or do you try again?

Even if you have been successful in the past, this is no time to sit back, smug and secure. It is time to say, "Hey, I can be anything I want to be." Because you really can. Where can you go from here? You have energy and experience, so what new goals can you set for the future?

189

THE THREE ELEMENTS OF EXCELLENCE

Attitude

Attitude is the first essential element of excellence. If you look at all the highly driven super-achievers you know and analyze what makes them tick, the first thing you will notice is their attitude. No matter how often or how badly they are put down by others or by circumstance, they hold on to a positive attitude about themselves. They are never intimidated.

How is your attitude today? You put your attitude on every morning just the same way you put your clothes on. If it is raining when you get up, are you going to let that change your day? Or are you going to focus on the things that count?

Motivation

The second element of excellence is motivation. You can't just want something; you have to want it *real bad*. You have to be totally focused on it, and driven, so that you forget about the obstacles, about the things you cannot do. I've seen so many people do things they supposedly can't do. It's like the old story about the bumble bee: it is not supposed to be able to fly, but it does. Its wings are too small for its heavy body, which isn't shaped for flying. But the bumble bee doesn't know that; it just flies.

Whenever I consider a deal I consider both my attitude toward it and my motivation to make it successful; if they aren't that strong — if I feel more strongly about another one — I pass on it.

Commitment

I met a man who worked for a cat-food company. It produced cat food that was more expensive than any of the other brands and I asked him how they managed to get twice the money that other manufacturers got for theirs. He started telling me how wonderful their product was: It was so good that at marketing meetings the president would stand up in front of everyone and eat the cat food. "Not only that," he said, "but we all eat it, too. The scientists and doctors — everyone tries it."

What they were doing was instilling commitment in these people, and that's the third element of excellence. "If it's good enough for me, it's good enough for your cat." Now, that's total commitment.

TEN GROUND RULES FOR EXCELLENCE

Below are my ground rules for excellence, the ones that work for me. Consider them and then add some of your own rules. But first, keep in mind two of the best-kept secrets in the world. These are things people generally won't tell you, but they are important to share with those around you.

Study the top movers and shakers and adapt their ideas to your industry.

Apply what Lee Iaccoca does to your industry, or Martin Luther King or Jimmy Pattison. Pick the current top operators you admire and determine how you can apply what they do to your business.

Let everything you do or say make a definitive statement about yourself.

We don't have enough heroes, so be a hero to your kids, your staff, your friends. Everything from your car and your clothes to your friends and your office should be an expression of your leadership, a message you want to pass on to others by example.

1. *You must have a mission.* A mission can electrify you and dynamically charge your staff, your family, your friends. When you focus on a mission you can affect the lives of those around you positively. That is the secret behind every successful person: they are just ordinary people with a mission. What is your mission?

2. *Know your customer.* It sounds simple, but how many of us really do it? Do you know where he lives, whether he has kids, what his likes and dislikes are? In order to do excellent business with him you must be able to see him through his eyes.

3. *Know your competitors.* You have to know everything, including what they discussed at their last board meeting, to survive. Some time ago I heard the president of Kodak make a presentation to the New York Stock Exchange. He told them that they should invest in his company because the successful products they saw before them were not even invented three years ago. Soon, it will be two years or less before whatever it is you do is threatened by

someone else who has invented a way to do it better, more cheaply, or more efficiently. That's why you have to know what your competitors are doing.

4. *Develop an attention to detail*. When I first became a general sales manager, I was given all the bad, non-producing regions. When we went to our first conference, on the second day I was to have a meeting with the regional managers. On the first day I watched them, and developed a feeling for each of them. Then at midnight I went to the room where I was to make my speech the next morning, and I rearranged the name cards in the order I thought they should be in around the table for the best results. I stood in front of the room and imagined them all there, and what I would say to them. I got a feeling for the place and the group and the right way to approach them, and worked through my presentation in my head. It was that sort of attention to detail that helped to get me in the right frame of mind to motivate them.

5. *To be effective, excellence must be initiated from the top*. The boss sets the standards and is the role model. The day you don't want to be a role model anymore is the day you should resign. When I ran Century 21, there came a time when I decided that I did not want to be the role model and be there every day, and I got myself a full-time CEO. When I went in, I was just in the way: I structured the company so that it didn't need me, and I only communicated with one person. But at McDonald's, for instance, Canadian President George Cohon has a religion called McDonald's, and he is everywhere; that's

why his company is so unbelievably successful. He's still keen to be the role model, and all his employees have the company in their blood. Do you have your company in your blood?

6. *Once you have decided on your mission, go for it as if your life depended on it.* Nothing electrifies your people more than when you paint a big picture for them, a grand design with all the routes for getting from here to there. Plan to be the best or the biggest or the finest or most professional, and then just fly with it, like a plane taking off. People get charged up when you make them feel part of something big. Do you do that with your staff?

7. *If it is possible, delegate.* As you move higher in management, you have to learn to discriminate every day between those things that you should look after yourself and those that you should let go of. Use any busy person as an example, but think to yourself, "Would Jimmy Pattison do this?" Ninety percent of what you do could be delegated — other people can do it. They can do it better if you just leave them alone. Tap their potential, expect the best of them, and they will rise to the occasion. The task may not be done the way you would do it, but it will get done.

8. *Watch out for the man with the monkeys on his shoulders.* That's what I call staffers who come to me with problems. You need to keep yourself clear of day-to-day problems by recognizing when people are coming toward you with monkeys on their shoulders. The key is to remember that monkeys can't jump more than three feet, so you must back up,

and keep backing up. You ask them if they have spoken to the manager in charge of that area. If you have organized your place properly, responsibility for all problems clearly falls on the shoulders of your managers. The rule is never to answer the question, never ask for details; just point them in the right direction.

9. *Before you get into any new project, ask yourself, "What is the worst thing that can happen to me?"* If the worst thing is not acceptable, don't get into the project. You'll save yourself a lot of aggravation that way.

10. *The second question to ask before getting into a business or project is, "Is it fun and is it profitable?"* It has to be both, not one or the other. You have to care for the people you are getting involved with, and enjoy their company. No amount of money is worth putting up with people who drive you crazy, or people you don't trust. There has to be pleasure along with the profit, and vice versa.

THE CONCEPT OF EXCELLENCE: A PRACTICAL SIX-STEP PROCESS FOR BOTTOM-LINE RESULTS

Complete the following six exercises as fully and frankly as possible. Take as much time as you need, perhaps allowing a day for each item, jotting ideas down as they occur to you during the day; or set aside some time to do it all.

1. Identify all your company's current strengths, advantages and accomplishments.

2. Define specifically all your company's objectives and time frames for achieving them.

3. Determine specific skills, talents or resources requiring further development.

4. Define your priorities in chronological sequence.

5. Evaluate your current status and progress in each of the above priorities.

6. Determine the specific actions and disciplines to be performed daily to achieve those priorities and to further develop the skills and resources listed under item three.

Your Implementation Plan

1. Schedule an executive-level planning meeting at your company. Review the above six items and circulate a copy of your answers. Ask participants to suggest alterations.

2. Select the concepts that best fit your company and collectively set goals, objectives and timetables.

3. Request that all executives or managers present an outline of programs for excellence within their departments. At your next meeting, review, amend and approve these plans.

4. Use these departmental plans to prepare an overall company-wide plan for excellence.

5. The master plan should be distributed to management, employees, customers, bankers, stockbrokers, parents, family and friends.

6. Establish a recognition-and-reward system for performance of excellence as measured by the plan.

Product Excellence

Become the best by comparison. Again, on a separate sheet of paper elaborate on the following six key points.

1. Define your products.

2. Specify the market you specialize in.

3. Name the current competitors in those markets.

4. Specify the decisions that must be made, by priority, about the marketplace and your company's place in it.

5. Assess how well you measure up to customer expectations.

6. Name priorities for implementation of improvement in reaching the market and satisfying customers.

Support Service Excellence

A product is only as good as the professionals who represent it. Give this list to your various departments and have them work on it separately. Then call a meeting of all of them to see what they came up with, and develop a master plan using the best results.

1. Identify everyone in your organization who may possibly come in contact with customers.

2. Define clearly the role and responsibility of each employee as it relates to customers.

3. Write a short corporate credo that defines the relationship between employees and customers.

4. Devise a reward-and-compensation system for excellence in customer service.

Excellence in Customer Service

Think of your customer as a partner in your business. Then try the exercise below.

1. Select a group of your six best customers to participate in a three-hour Focus Group Session.

2. Define specific products, services or issues to be discussed.

3. Determine the Top Ten Performance Characteristics to measure overall effectiveness.

4. Provide the group with a Performance Review Form to assess current company status and make suggestions for improvement.

5. Determine Action Steps necessary to ensure customer satisfaction.

Excellence in Employee Relations

Respect for the individual is the most important component of a successful business. Consider the following aspects of employee relations.

1. Define the key issues influencing employee morale and internal motivation.

2. Develop an annual Employee Attitude Survey.

3. Test the survey on a sampling of employees in various departments and levels.

4. Launch the survey in phases, by level of management.

5. Compile the results and suggestions and provide the findings in the form of a bulletin.

Excellence in Long-Term Goals

Now we get to some personal assessment, starting with your career.

1. Where would you like to be, professionally, ten years from today?

2. Which profession or career track would provide you with the best opportunities?

3. What talents, skills or credentials must you develop to achieve this goal?

4. What must you do over the next three months to initiate this momentum?

5. How will you reward yourself when you achieve your goal?

The Perception of Success

Step back from your career now and assess your personal situation: decide what is really important to you. How would you complete the statements below?

1. To me, success means:

2. The type of life I intend to live once I achieve my goal is:

3. The type of people I will associate with will be:

4. My typical business day agenda will be:

5. The types of personal rewards I will choose will include:

Your Implementation Checklist

Choose three of the points below — make a list and put your name and the date on it. Glance at the list regularly to remind yourself of what you've resolved to do. In a couple of months, assess your performance and your selections. Pick a few other points you would like to try and start again.

— Think in terms of being your own boss.
— Do what you do so well that people enthusiastically refer others to you.
— Inspire others by your example.
— Build your reputation on honesty, integrity, quality and superb service.
— Aim for excellence in your field.
— Support others in achieving their goals.
— Develop influential friendships worldwide.
— Do things that are extraordinary and nearly impossible.
— Take total responsibility for your past, present and future experiences.
— Do and say things that benefit all concerned.
— Be open to new ideas, relationships and experiences.
— Realize that all events happen for the best.
— Take calculated risks to get ahead.
— Read books by and about exciting people you admire.
— Simplify your life; have more fun per hour.

— Accept people the way they are.
— Forgive and love everyone.
— Do what you feel is best, no matter what other people think of you.
— Give something away daily: a postcard, letter, gift, smile, hug or compliment.
— Collect pictures of what you want to be, do and have in life.
— Do not criticize, condemn or complain.
— Dress to look and feel great.
— Collect quotes that motivate you.
— Speak and write only positive words.
— Learn something new every day.
— Avoid saying: can't, hard, difficult.
— Keep your home, office and car clean, neat and organized.
— Take time out to relax.
— Act as if all your goals are already accomplished.
— Constantly escalate your goals.

Index